Reach HIGHER

Practice Book

NATIONAL GEOGRAPHIC LEARNING

Australia • Brazil • Mexico • Singapore • United Kingdom • United States

National Geographic Learning,
a Cengage Company

Reach Higher Practice Book 6A

Publisher, Content-based English: Erik Gundersen

Associate Director, R&D: Barnaby Pelter

Senior Development Editors:
  Jacqueline Eu
  Ranjini Fonseka
  Kelsey Zhang

Development Editor: Rayne Ngoi

Director of Global Marketing: Ian Martin

Heads of Regional Marketing:
  Charlotte Ellis (Europe, Middle East and Africa)
  Kiel Hamm (Asia)
  Irina Pereyra (Latin America)

Product Marketing Manager: David Spain

Senior Production Controller: Tan Jin Hock

Senior Media Researcher (Covers): Leila Hishmeh

Senior Designer: Lisa Trager

Director, Operations: Jason Seigel

Operations Support:
  Rebecca Barbush
  Drew Robertson
  Caroline Stephenson
  Nicholas Yeaton

Manufacturing Planner: Mary Beth Hennebury

Publishing Consultancy and Composition:
  MPS North America LLC

© 2020 Cengage Learning, Inc.

ALL RIGHTS RESERVED. No part of this work covered by the copyright herein may be reproduced or distributed in any form or by any means, except as permitted by U.S. copyright law, without the prior written permission of the copyright owner.

"National Geographic", "National Geographic Society" and the Yellow Border Design are registered trademarks of the National Geographic Society ® Marcas Registradas

For permission to use material from this text or product, submit all requests online at **cengage.com/permissions**
Further permissions questions can be emailed to **permissionrequest@cengage.com**

ISBN-13: 978-0-357-36706-3

National Geographic Learning
200 Pier Four Blvd
Boston, MA 02210
USA

Locate your local office at **international.cengage.com/region**

Visit National Geographic Learning online at **ELTNGL.com**
Visit our corporate website at **www.cengage.com**

Printed in China
Print Number: 08   Print Year: 2023

Contents

Unit 1: The Power of Choice

Part 1

Unit 1 Concept Map 1.1
Thinking Map: Main Idea Diagram 1.2
Grammar: Nouns 1.3
Key Points Reading:
   "The Vision of the Sightless" 1.4
Grammar: Subjects and Predicates 1.6
Reread and Retell: Main Idea Diagram 1.7
Fluency: Intonation 1.8
Reading Options: Reflection Journal 1.9
Respond and Extend: Comparison Chart 1.10
Grammar: Complete Sentences 1.11
Close Reading: "A Work in Progress" 1.12

Part 2

Thinking Map: Character-and-Plot Chart 1.15
Grammar:
   Verb Agreement with Simple Subjects 1.16
Key Points Reading: "Hot off the Press" 1.17
Grammar: Compound Subjects 1.18
Vocabulary: Apply Word Knowledge 1.19
Reread and Retell: Character-and-Plot Chart ... 1.20
Fluency: Expression 1.21
Reading Options: Dialogue Journal 1.22
Respond and Extend: Character Chart 1.23
Grammar: Subject-Verb Agreement 1.24
Close Reading:
   "The Spark of Determination" 1.25
Writing Project: Write a Personal Narrative 1.28

Unit 2: Survival

Part 1

Unit 2 Concept Map 2.1
Thinking Map: Main Idea Chart 2.2
Grammar: Subject Pronouns 2.3
Key Points Reading:
   "Deception: Formula for Survival" 2.4
Grammar: Object Pronouns 2.5
Reread and Retell: Main Idea Chart 2.6
Fluency: Phrasing 2.7
Reading Options: Fact Cards 2.8
Respond and Extend: Comparison Chart 2.9
Grammar: Subject and Object Pronouns 2.10
Close Reading: "Living Nightmares" 2.11

Part 2

Thinking Map: Character Chart 2.14
Grammar: Possessive Nouns 2.15
Key Points Reading: "Hatchet" 2.16
Grammar: Possessive
   Adjectives and Pronouns 2.17
Reread and Retell: Character Chart 2.18
Fluency: Expression 2.19
Reading Options: Prediction Chart 2.20
Respond and Extend: Comparison Chart 2.21
Grammar: Possessive
   Adjectives and Pronouns 2.22
Close Reading:
   "The Girl Who Fell from the Sky" 2.23
Writing Project: Write an Expository Report ... 2.26

Unit 3: Digging Up the Past

Part 1

Unit 3 Concept Map 3.1
Thinking Map: Double Time Line 3.2
Grammar: Present Progressive Verbs 3.3
Key Points Reading: "Valley of the Kings" 3.4
Grammar: Past and Future Progressive 3.5
Reread and Retell: Double Time Line 3.6
Fluency: Phrasing 3.7
Reading Options: K-W-L-Q Chart 3.8
Respond and Extend:
   Comparison Chart 3.9
Grammar: Progressive Tenses 3.10
Close Reading: "Animals Everlasting" 3.11

Part 2

Thinking Map: Plot Diagram 3.14
Grammar: Contractions 3.15
Key Points Reading: "Ahmes's Journal" 3.16
Grammar: Modals 3.17
Vocabulary: Apply Word Knowledge 3.18
Reread and Retell: Plot Diagram 3.19
Fluency: Expression 3.20
Reading Options: Reflection Journal 3.21
Respond and Extend: Comparison Chart 3.22
Grammar: Modals 3.23
Close Reading: "The Golden Goblet" 3.24
Writing Project: Write a Research Report 3.27

Unit 4: Our Diverse Earth

Part 1

Unit 4 Concept Map 4.1
Thinking Map: Viewpoint Chart 4.2
Grammar: Adjectives 4.3
Key Points Reading: "A Natural Balance" 4.4
Grammar: Adverbs 4.6
Reread and Retell: Viewpoint Chart 4.7
Fluency: Phrasing 4.8
Reading Options: Viewpoint Chart 4.9
Respond and Extend: Venn Diagram 4.10
Grammar: Adjectives and Adverbs 4.11
Close Reading: "Mireya Mayor" 4.12

Part 2

Thinking Map: Character Description Chart 4.15
Grammar: Present Participles 4.16
Key Points Reading: "If Trees Could Talk" 4.17
Grammar: Past Participles 4.19
Reread and Explain:
   Character Description Chart 4.20
Fluency: Expression 4.21
Reading Options: Double-Entry Log 4.22
Respond and Extend: Comparison Chart 4.23
Grammar: Participial Phrases 4.24
Close Reading: "The Super Trees" 4.25
Writing Project: Write an Argument 4.28
Photographic Credits 4.32

Name _____ Date _____

Unit Concept Map

The Power of Choice

Make a concept map with the answers to the Big Question: How do choices affect who you are?

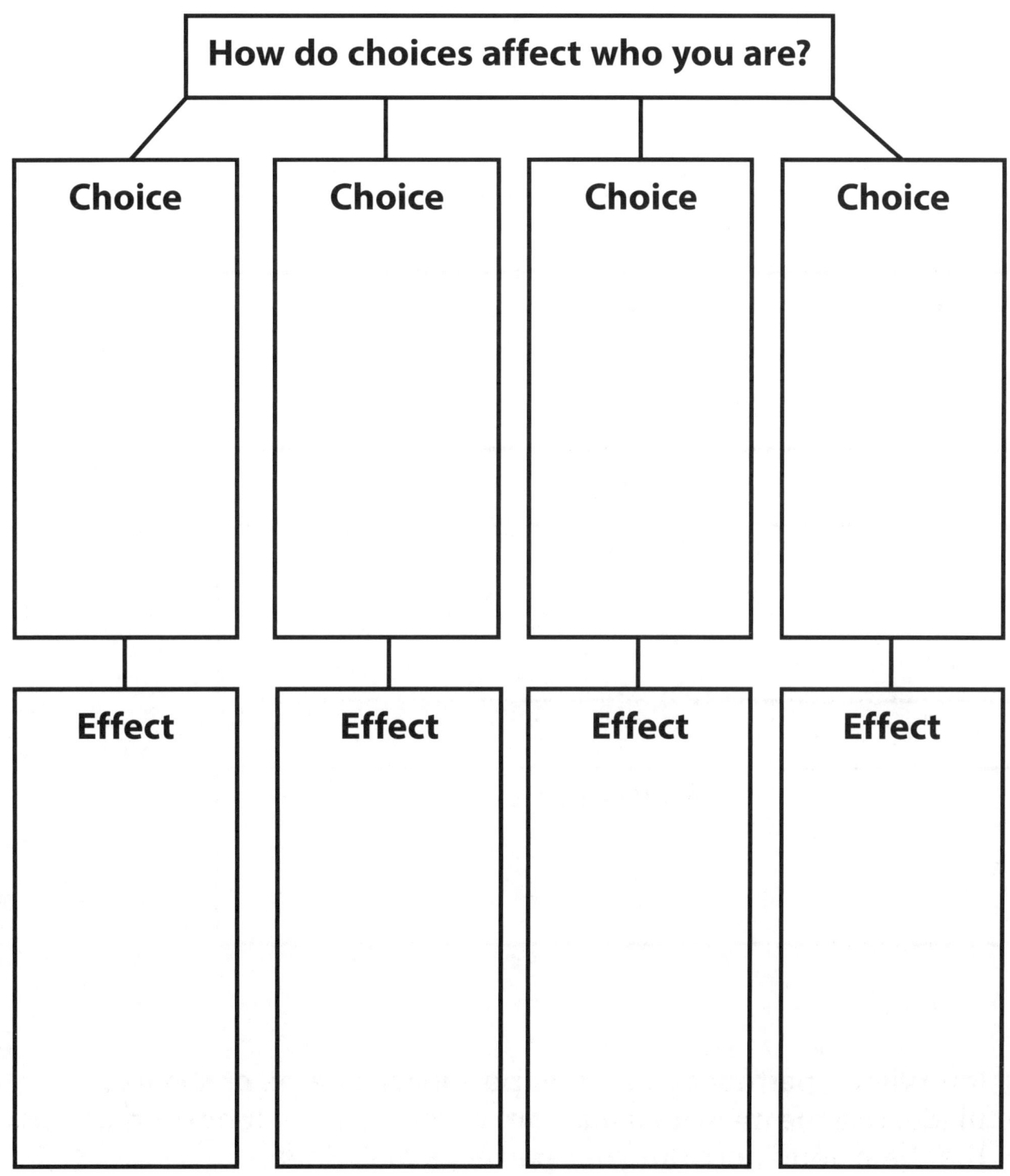

Name _____   Date _____

Thinking Map

Main Idea

Fill in a main idea diagram with supporting details that help you figure out the main idea.

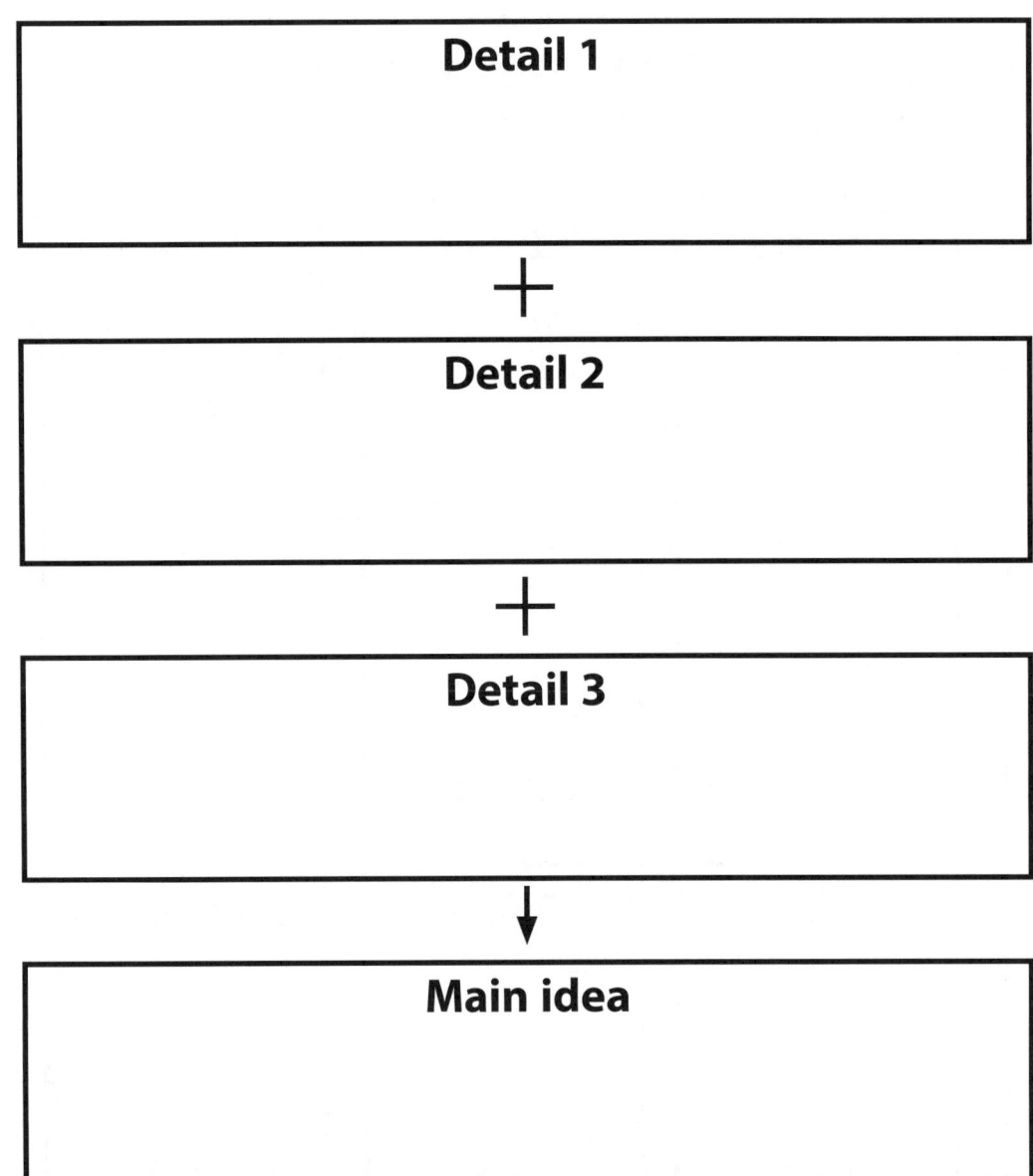

Interview a partner about an important choice he or she has made. Use the main idea diagram to record the supporting details that help you figure out your partner's main idea.

1.2 Unit 1 | The Power of Choice

Name _____ Date _____

Grammar

Make Nouns Plural

1. Play with one or two other players.
2. Use a paper clip, eraser, or other small object as a game marker, and place it on **START**.
3. Flip a coin to move ahead. Heads = one space; tails = two spaces.
4. Read the noun on the space where you land. Write its plural form or write "noncount" or "collective."
5. If the other players agree with you, stay where you are. If not, go back one space. If you disagree with the others, check the spelling in a dictionary.
6. Take turns. The first person to reach **FINISH** is the winner.

START	jacket	fox	grass	fly
				wish
cow	mouse	tomato	water	branch
herd				
shoe	woman	encounter	knife	FINISH

1.3   Unit 1 | The Power of Choice

Key Points Reading

"The Vision of the Sightless"

Listen as your teacher reads. Follow with your finger.

Louis Braille was born in 1809 in a small town in France. He became blind as a child. His parents saw his potential and wanted him to have a full and independent life. They helped him apply for a scholarship to attend the National Institute for Blind Children in Paris. Louis was intelligent and had a positive attitude, and he worked hard at school.

Louis did well in his studies and also in his music lessons. He helped his classmates, too.

When he was 12, he became interested in Charles Barbier's night-writing system, which Barbier had developed to help soldiers communicate quietly at night during a war. The system consisted of 12 dots embossed on paper, with the dots arranged differently to represent different sounds.

"The Vision of the Sightless" (continued)

Louis simplified Barbier's system. He decided to use just 6 dots to represent letters instead of sounds. He thought those who were blind could use it to read by touch. However, his school did not adopt this new system easily. Officials thought it was too difficult and too expensive to change the way they did things.

Louis continued to advocate his new system. He published a book in braille and pushed for his new system to become adopted by schools. Little by little, it was accepted.

Today, braille is used by blind people all over the world, in many languages. Louis was not discouraged by his disability. Instead, he used his abilities to change many people's lives.

Name _____   Date _____

Grammar

Ray Charles

Grammar Rules Subjects and Predicates

1. A **complete sentence** expresses a complete thought. A sentence fragment does not express a complete thought.
2. The **complete subject** includes all the words that tell about the subject. The **simple subject** is the most important noun.
3. The **complete predicate** includes the verb and all the other words in the predicate. The **simple predicate** is the main verb.

Read each item. Draw one line under each complete subject and two lines under each complete predicate. If the item is a fragment, write S if it is missing a subject or P if it is missing a predicate.

1. Ray Charles's mother passed away when he was 15 years old.

2. Demonstrated an extraordinary ability for music.

3. Ray's disability did not hold him back.

4. His studies at the Florida School for the Deaf and the Blind.

5. Loss of sight does not mean a loss of intelligence or will.

6. Ray became a musician who shaped soul music.

Name _____ Date _____

Reread and Retell

"The Vision of the Sightless"

Use a main idea diagram to record important details that lead to the main idea.

Detail 1
Louis had an accident as a child.

+

Detail 2

+

Detail 3

+

Detail 4

↓

Main idea

Use the diagram to restate the main idea to a partner. Explain how the details helped you figure out the main idea.

Name _____   Date _____

Fluency

"The Vision of the Sightless"

Use this passage to practice reading with proper intonation.

It would still take a few years for his school to adopt braille as the	15
formal system of instruction, but it eventually happened. It was not only	27
adopted by his school but, little by little, became accepted in many places	40
beyond France, revolutionizing the educational system for the blind. Thanks	50
to braille, blind people could easily learn and communicate with each other	62
without the help of sighted people. Blind people started reading more and	74
using braille to write their personal stories.	81
Braille became universally accepted as the code of reading and writing	92
for the blind shortly after Louis Braille passed away. The system has been	105
adapted for use in many different languages, and there are now electronic	117
machines that simplify writing in braille for the blind. Today, technology has	129
provided more alternatives for the blind, but braille is still a very practical	142
solution for the visually impaired.	147

From "The Vision of the Sightless," page 20

Intonation

1. ☐ Does not change pitch.
2. ☐ Changes pitch, but does not match content.
3. ☐ Changes pitch to match some of the content.
4. ☐ Changes pitch to match all of the content.

Accuracy and Rate Formula

Use the formula to measure a reader's accuracy and rate while reading aloud.

_____ − _____ = _____
words attempted   number of errors   words correct per minute
in one minute   (wcpm)

1.8   Unit 1 | The Power of Choice

Name _____ Date _____

Reading Options

"A Work in Progress"

Complete this reflection journal as you read the speech.

Page	My question	The answer

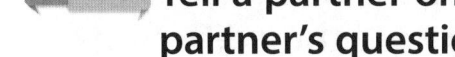 Tell a partner one of your questions. Then try to answer your partner's question.

Name _____ Date _____

Respond and Extend

Compare Main Ideas

Use a comparison chart to compare the two selections.

	"The Vision of the Sightless"	"A Work in Progress"
Genre	biography	
Main idea		
Main character's choice		

 Take turns with a partner. Discuss the main ideas of each text. How are the main characters' choices similar? How are they different?

1.10   Unit 1 | The Power of Choice

Name _____ Date _____

Grammar

Amanda's Idea

Grammar Rules Complete Sentences

1. A sentence expresses a complete thought.
2. The **complete subject** includes all the words that tell about the subject. The **simple subject** is the most important noun.
3. The **complete predicate** includes the verb and all the other words in the predicate. The **simple predicate** is the main verb.

Read each sentence. Draw a line between the complete subject and the complete predicate. Then draw one line under the simple subject and two lines under the simple predicate.

1. Amanda's grandmother   invited Amanda to lunch on Saturday.

2. Then Amanda's friend   asked her to a beach party on the same day.

3. Both of the activities   sounded like fun.

4. Amanda   wasn't sure what to do.

5. Then, in a flash of inspiration, Amanda   had an idea.

6. Clever Amanda   took her grandmother to lunch at the beach party.

   Tell a partner about a time when you had to make a choice between two activities. After each sentence, stop and have your partner identify the simple subject and simple predicate in the sentence. Then, switch roles.

1.11   Unit 1 | The Power of Choice

Name _____ Date _____

Close Reading

from "A Work in Progress," page 29

Analyze the text below with your teacher and make notes.

1. When I was fourteen it was Easter Sunday, and I was gonna be wearing a dress that I had purchased with my own money—the first thing I ever bought that wasn't on sale. Momentous event; you never forget it. I'd had a paper route since I was twelve, and I went to The Limited, and I bought this dress that I thought was the height of sophistication—sleeveless safari dress, belted, hits at the knee.

2. Coming downstairs into the living room, I see my father waiting to take us to church. He takes one look at me, and he says, "That doesn't look right. Go upstairs and change."

3. I was like "What? My super-classy dress? What are you talking about? It's the best thing I own."

4. He said, "No, you can see the knee joint when you walk. It doesn't look right. It's inappropriate to go out like that. Go change."

5. And I think something snapped in me. I refused to change.

Name _____ Date _____

Close Reading

from "A Work in Progress," page 30

Make notes as you read the paragraphs below. Then answer the questions on page 1.14.

1. I decided I wanted to be the fastest woman in the world on prosthetic legs and I was lucky enough to arrive in track at just the right time to be the first person to get these radical sprinting legs modeled after the hind leg of a cheetah, the fastest thing that runs—woven carbon fiber. I was able to set three world records with those legs. And they made no attempt at approximating humanness.

2. Then I get these incredibly lifelike silicone legs—hand-painted, capillaries, veins. And, hey, I can be as tall as I wanna be, so I get different legs for different heights. I don't have to shave. I can wear open-toed shoes in the winter. And most importantly, I can opt out of the cankles I most certainly would've inherited genetically.

Name _____ Date _____

Close Reading

from "A Work in Progress" (continued)

Reread and then annotate the text to answer these questions.

Reread paragraph 1.

1. Break the first sentence into three or more ideas. Highlight each idea.

   Then write a summary of the sentences in the margin.

2. Underline and unpack: "And they made no attempt at approximating humanness." What does "they" refer to? Find another way to say "made no attempt at." What does "approximating humanness" mean? Put these meanings together, and write the meaning in the margin.

Reread paragraph 2.

3. Underline "silicone." Use context clues to figure out the meaning of *silicone*.

4. Summarize the benefit of prosthetic legs. Highlight text evidence.

5. Underline and unpack: "And most importantly, I can opt out of the cankles I most certainly would've inherited genetically."

6. Review the paragraph. The details in this paragraph are about things Aimee can do with her prosthetic legs. Write the main idea in the margin.

Name _____ Date _____

Thinking Map

Characters and Plot

Complete a character-and-plot chart.

Character	Plot event	Response

Tell a partner about an important decision that someone you know made. Describe how you responded to the decision. Your partner completes a character-and-plot chart and uses it to retell your story.

Name _____ Date _____

Grammar

A New Year Tradition

Grammar Rules Verb Agreement with Simple Subjects

1. Use a singular action verb or form of **be** with a **singular subject**:
   Examples: **Mom bakes** bread. **The bread is** sweet.
2. Use a plural action verb or form of **be** with a **plural subject**:
   Examples: **We cut** the bread. **The slices are** warm.
3. For the pronoun **I**, use a plural action verb and a special form of **be**:
   Examples: **I take** a piece. **I am** excited.
4. For the pronoun **you**, use a plural action verb and the plural form of **be**:
   Examples: **You take** a piece. **You are** excited.

Read each item. Underline the simple subject. Circle the verb that completes the sentence.

1. The bakers (wrap / wraps) a coin in tin foil.

2. They (hide / hides) the coin in the New Year bread.

3. My dad (cut / cuts) our New Year bread into slices.

4. You (is / are) lucky to get the coin.

5. I (find / finds) the coin in my slice this year.

6. I (is / am) the lucky one!

   Use these verbs to write sentences with simple subjects: *is, are, am, eat, eats.*

Name _____ Date _____

Key Points Reading

"Hot off the Press"

Listen as your teacher reads. Follow with your finger.

1. Mia is excited to join the school newspaper. She is assigned the role of website assistant. Mia takes notes for a story about a special lunch line in the school cafeteria for students with food allergies.

2. Olivia, a senior student editor, writes the story to make it sound like the cafeteria is doing something harmful, when it's really doing something helpful. Olivia thinks readers will be more interested in this type of story.

3. Mia knows it's wrong to publish an article that is not true. She makes the brave decision to speak up and say she won't publish it. Mrs. Mendoza asks her to rewrite the article. The new article is a big hit!

Name _____ Date _____

Grammar

School Newspaper

Grammar Rules: Compound Subjects

A **compound subject** has two or more simple subjects. Use a plural verb when two subjects are joined by **and**.

When the subjects are joined by **or**, look at the last noun.
- If it is singular, use a singular verb.
- If it is plural, use a plural verb.

Examples: The students **and** Mia smile.
Mia **and** the students smile.

Examples: The editors **or** Mrs. Mendoza sits here.
Mrs. Mendoza **or** the editors sit here.

Read each sentence. Circle the word that joins the simple subjects. Then choose the correct form of the verb and underline it.

1. Mia and some other students (write/writes) for the newspaper.

2. My friend and I (is/are) curious about the secret lunch line.

3. Olivia or Marcus (type/types) the article.

4. The students and Mrs. Mendoza (ask/asks) a lot of questions.

5. Mia or the students (answer/answers) them.

6. Questions and answers (help/helps) us understand new things.

Write compound subjects with **and** and **or**. Then write verbs for each compound subject.

1.18   Unit 1 | The Power of Choice

Name _____ Date _____

Vocabulary

Vocabulary Bingo

Play Bingo using the Key Words from this unit.

Name _____ Date _____

Reread and Retell

"Hot off the Press"

Record events from the story using a character-and-plot chart.

Character	Plot event	Response
Mrs. Mendoza	asks Mia to rewrite the article	

 Use the chart to retell the story to a partner.

Fluency

"Hot off the Press"

Use this passage to practice reading with proper expression.

Mrs. Jackson frowned. "Mia? Do you have food allergies?"	9
"Uh, no," I said. "I'm from the *Beacon*."	17
She smiled. "Writing a story about the special diet line."	27
"Special diet?" I asked.	31
Mrs. Jackson nodded. "For kids who are sensitive to certain foods."	42
She explained that the school had started providing a separate line for	54
students who didn't have a tolerance for foods like milk, nuts, or wheat.	67
"Food allergies can be dangerous," she said.	74
Andre laughed. "Mrs. Jackson doesn't want to accidentally poison me	84
with a peanut."	87
I took pages of notes about the special diet line.	97

From "Hot off the Press," page 50

Expression

- [1] ☐ Does not read with feeling.
- [2] ☐ Reads with some feeling, but does not match content.
- [3] ☐ Reads with appropriate feeling for most content.
- [4] ☐ Reads with appropriate feeling for all content.

Accuracy and Rate Formula

Use the formula to measure a reader's accuracy and rate while reading aloud.

_____ − _____ = _____
words attempted   number of errors   words correct per minute
in one minute   (wcpm)

1.21   Unit 1 | The Power of Choice

Name _____ Date _____

Reading Options

"The Spark of Determination"

Complete a dialogue journal as you read the biography.

What I think	What my partner thinks
Page _____ _____ _____ _____	_____ _____ _____ _____
Page _____ _____ _____ _____	_____ _____ _____ _____
Page _____ _____ _____ _____	_____ _____ _____ _____
Page _____ _____ _____ _____	_____ _____ _____ _____

 Tell a partner your thoughts about each page. Then ask your partner to share his or her thoughts.

Name _____ Date _____

Respond and Extend

Compare Characters

Use a character chart to compare two characters from the selections.

	"Hot off the Press"	"The Spark of Determination"
Narrator or main character	Mia	Sparky
Problem		
Thoughts and feelings		
Choices		
Actions and responses		

Complete the chart with a partner. Then discuss the problems that each character faced and how they responded to it.

Name _____   Date _____

Grammar

Charles Schulz

Grammar Rules Subject-Verb Agreement

1. Use a singular verb with a singular subject.
2. Use a plural verb with a plural subject.
3. Use a plural verb if the subject is **I** or **you**.
4. When **and** joins two simple subjects, use a plural verb.
5. When **or** or **nor** joins two subjects, use a verb that agrees with the simple subject closest to it.

Read each sentence. Write the correct form of the verb in parentheses to agree with the subject.

1. Sparky's parents (be) good, hardworking people.

   _____

2. Sparky and his uncle (like) to read comics.

   _____

3. His friends or his teacher (tell) him he could be an artist.

   _____

4. Neither Disney nor the magazines (accept) his application.

   _____

▬▬ Say one sentence with a compound subject. Ask a partner to tell whether your subject and verb agree and correct your agreement if it is incorrect. Then trade roles.

1.24   Unit 1 | The Power of Choice

Name _____ Date _____

Close Reading

from "The Spark of Determination," page 59

Analyze the text below with your teacher and make notes.

1. He also had a lot of love for the family dogs. They had a black Boston Bull Terrier named Spooky, and then, after she passed away, a black and white mixed-breed dog named Spike, which was intelligent and fun to be around. But Sparky's true love was comic strips, and he grew up dreaming of one day being able to draw his own comics.

2. Inspired by that dream, Sparky, at age 14, drew the family dog, Spike, and he and his dad sent the picture to a magazine. They wrote about how Spike would eat all sorts of strange things, such as pins and razor blades. The magazine published the drawing, giving Sparky his first taste of success as a cartoonist.

3. In spite of this first small but happy achievement, Sparky's teenage years were not easy. He was shy and kept to himself a lot. Others perceived him as a good kid but also an anxious one. In his senior year, he decided to submit cartoons to his high school yearbook, but the student committee in charge did not publish them. Despite this disappointment, Sparky did not give up. He kept drawing. Drawing and cartoons remained his main hobby and ambition.

Name _____ Date _____

Close Reading

from "The Spark of Determination," page 60

Make notes as you read the paragraphs below. Then answer the questions on page 1.27.

1. At 18 years old, Sparky decided to take a course in drawing. He graduated from high school and started doing different jobs, but he could not stop thinking about the world of cartoons and illustrations. He sent his drawings and ideas to different magazines, always getting rejection letters. He also applied to work as an animator for Walt Disney, but he was turned down from that, too. He then enlisted in the army.

2. After serving as a sergeant for the United States Army in World War II, Sparky came home determined to do what he loved. He was finally offered a job that was more in line with his artistic inclinations. He became an art instructor for Art Instruction Schools, Inc.—the same school where he had previously taken his drawing course. Things were looking up, but making his own comic was still his dream.

3. He did not give up. He kept writing and trying to sell his cartoons. He drew about things he knew until finally, he sold a strip called *Li'l Folks by Sparky*. This strip was about a young boy like the one he had been: shy and with little success, owner of a black and white dog he loved.

Name _____ Date _____

Close Reading

from "The Spark of Determination" (continued)

Reread and annotate the passage to answer these questions.

Reread paragraphs 1–3.

1. The author writes, "But Sparky's true love was comic strips." Underline examples of this in these paragraphs.

2. Sparky had many failures and successes throughout his life before he finally became a famous cartoonist. Find examples of his failures and successes in the text. Write margin notes describing them in your own words.

Reread paragraph 3.

3. Reread the sentence, "He drew about things he knew...." Highlight an example of this in the text. Explain how drawing what he knew contributed to his success.

Name _____ Date _____

Writing Project

Organization

Writing is organized when it is easy to follow. All the ideas make sense together and flow from one idea to the next in an order that fits the writer's audience and purpose.

	Is the personal narrative organized?	Does the writing flow?
4 Wow!	❑ The writing has a clear beginning, middle, and end. The organization fits the purpose of a personal narrative.	❑ The order of events makes sense because the writer uses transition words. The narrative flows smoothly and logically.
3 Ahh.	❑ The writing is mostly organized with a beginning, middle, and end. A few story events are out of order.	❑ The writing is mostly smooth, but it needs transition words in a few places.
2 Hmm.	❑ The writing has a beginning and an end, but many story events are out of order.	❑ The writing flows smoothly in some places but is hard to follow in others.
1 Huh?	❑ The writing is not organized. Maybe the writer forgot to use a sequence chain to plan.	❑ I can't tell what the writer wants to say because the writing jumps around too much.

© Cengage Learning, Inc.

Name _____ Date _____

Writing Project

Sequence Chain

Complete a sequence chain for your personal narrative.

Beginning

Middle

End

Unit 1 | The Power of Choice

Name _____   Date _____

Writing Project

Revise

Use revision marks to make changes to this paragraph. Look for:

- a logical sequence of events
- transition words
- vivid language and descriptive details

Revision Marks	
∧	Add
℘	Take out
∧̂	Insert comma
◯⌒∧	Move to here

A New Sport for Quinn

Last fall, Mom and Dad told me to try a new sport.

So I read about different sports and made a list of questions.

Finally, I signed up for the swim team. I attended events where coaches answered my questions. I thought about joining each team.

Rewrite your revised paragraph on the lines.

_____
_____
_____
_____

1.30   Unit 1 | The Power of Choice

Name _____   Date _____

Writing Project

Edit and Proofread

Use revision marks to edit and proofread these paragraphs. Look for:

- irregular plural nouns
- subject-verb agreement
- complete sentences with capitalization and end marks

Revision Marks	
∧	Add
℘	Take out
⊙	Insert period
≡	Capitalize
/	Make lowercase

A New Sport for Quinn (continued)

I was nervous but excited to be on the swim team. Both Coach Kate and Coach Tom has a lot of experience. At practice, the coachs demonstrated the strokes. I watched and imitated them Coach Tom timed me. Counted my strokes. Before long, my arms and legs was much stronger. My foots kicked hard, churning the water and moving me along at a good pace.

My brothers and my parentes came to cheer for me at my first meet. I were swimming in the 50-yard freestyle. first, I put on my cap and adjusted my goggles. Next, I took my place on the starting block then, the starting whistle blew. Like a rocket, I dove in and swam harder than I ever had before. To my surprise, I won! My family and coaches cheered. My teammates yelled. gave me high-fives. A great moment. I am so glad I joined the swim team.

Name _____ Date _____

Unit Concept Map

Survival

Make a concept map with the answers to the Big Question:
What does it take to survive?

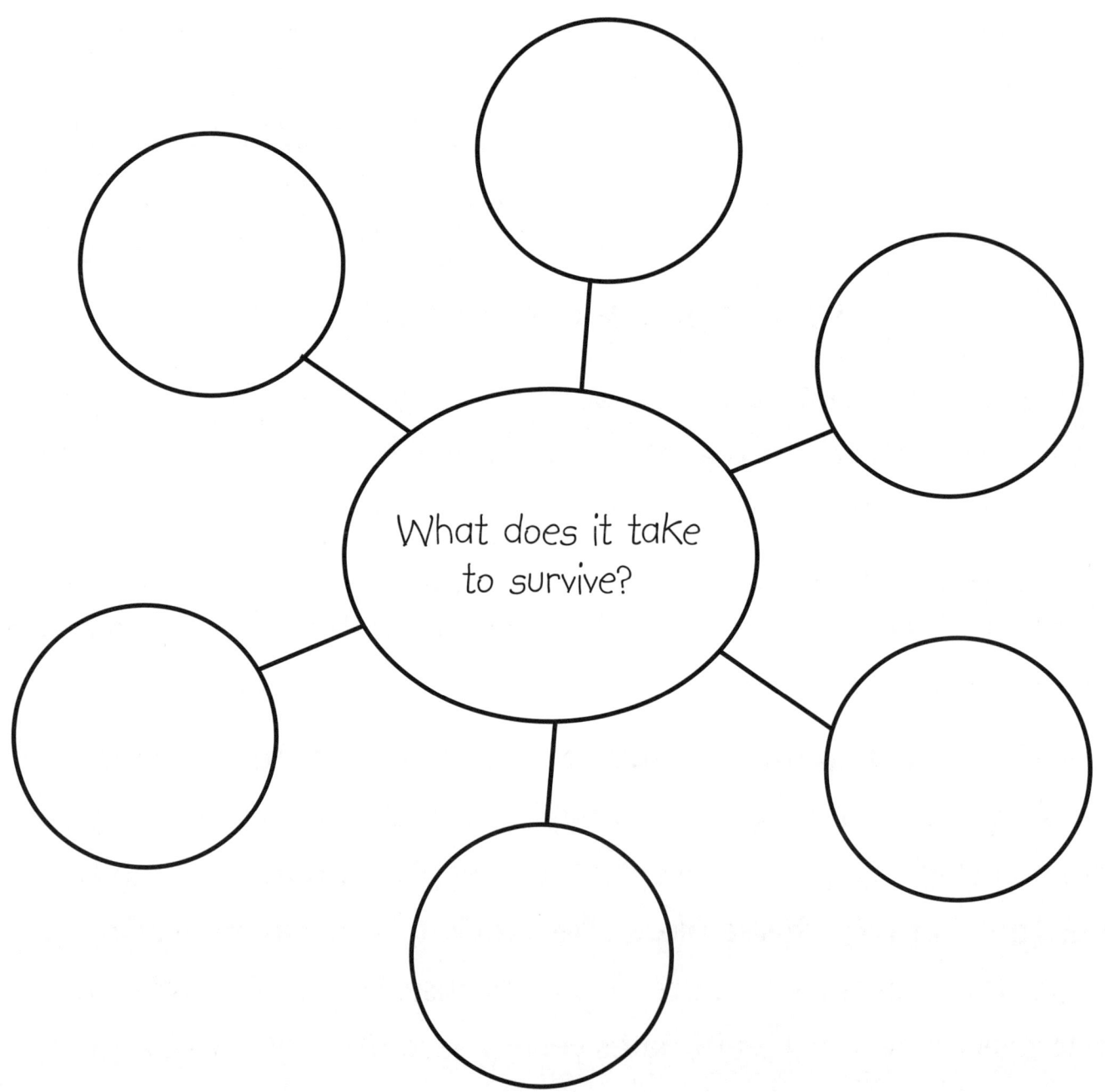

2.1 — Unit 2 | Survival

Name _____ Date _____

Thinking Map

Main Idea and Details

Fill in the main idea chart as a partner tells you about two animals that have amazing abilities.

Section head	Important details	Main idea of section

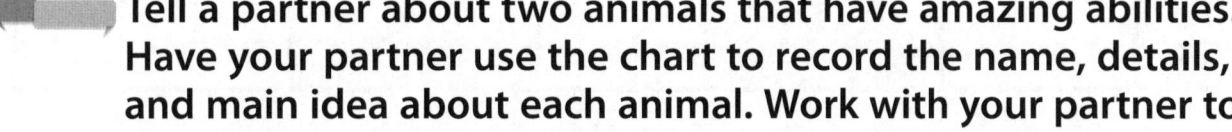 Tell a partner about two animals that have amazing abilities. Have your partner use the chart to record the name, details, and main idea about each animal. Work with your partner to determine a main idea that is true about both animals.

2.2

Unit 2 | Survival

Name _____   Date _____

Grammar

Name the Subject Pronoun

Directions:

1. Play with a partner. Put your marker on START.
2. Flip a coin to move. Heads = one space; tails = two spaces.
3. Read the noun on the space where you land. Write the subject pronoun that agrees with it. Then say that pronoun in a sentence.
4. If your partner agrees that your responses are correct, stay where you are. If not, go back one space. If you disagree, check with another pair of students.

START	Robert	Margie	leaf	Uncle Tony	Mrs. Sims
					photograph
trees	girl	Mr. Moriso	plants	Aunt Rosa	Granddad
brother					
Grandma	desert	caterpillar	sister	boys	FINISH

Unit 2 | Survival

Key Points Reading

"Deception: Formula for Survival"

Listen as your teacher reads. Follow with your finger.

❶

Some animals and plants use adaptation and deception to survive. Camouflage helps organisms blend into their surroundings. A yellow crab spider hides in a yellow flower. When the spider attacks, its prey does not see it. A looper sticks flower petals to its back. It blends with the flower and is safe from predators.

❷

Some organisms mimic other species. A good-tasting bug may mimic one that tastes bad. Its predators may avoid eating it. Animals may also mimic movements, smell, or even sound. One fly species beats its wings to sound like the wasp it resembles.

❸

Scientists study adaptations and survival. In one experiment, moths painted like bad-tasting butterflies fared better than moths painted like tasty ones. In nature, deception can be the key to one's survival.

Name _____ Date _____

Grammar

Object Pronouns: Spin and Speak

1. Play in a small group.
2. Take turns spinning the paper clip.
   - If you land on an object pronoun, say it in a sentence.
   - If you land on a noun, substitute an object pronoun for it. Then say the object pronoun in a sentence.
   - If you land on a subject pronoun, spin again.
3. If the other players agree that you used the pronoun correctly, give yourself one point.
4. The first player to get 10 points wins.

Make a Spinner

1. Place one loop of a paper clip over the center of the circle.
2. Push a sharp pencil through the loop and the paper.
3. Spin the paper clip around the pencil.

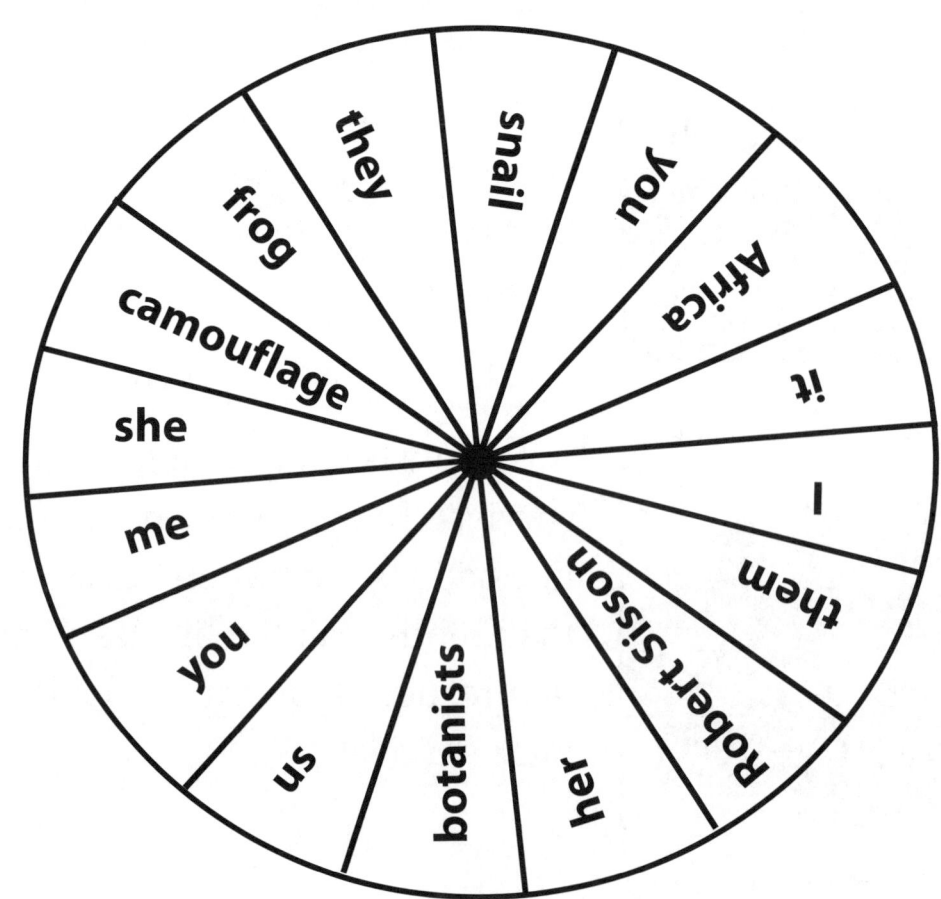

2.5

Unit 2 | Survival

Name _____ Date _____

Reread and Retell

"Deception: Formula for Survival"

Reread "Deception: Formula for Survival." Then fill in the main idea chart.

Section head	Important details	Main idea of section
Masters of Disguise (page 80)	1. Plants look like rocks. 2. 3.	Living things adapt to hide from predators.
	1. 2. 3.	

Fill in the information for your chosen section. Then summarize the section for a partner. As a team, use the information from both of your charts and what you read to determine the main idea for the entire selection.

2.6 Unit 2 | Survival

Name _____ Date _____

Fluency

"Deception: Formula for Survival"

Use this passage to practice reading with proper phrasing.

A successful mimic may not only look, feel, smell, and	10
move like its model, but it even may gear its life to the same	24
seasons in which its model operates. As mimics change to	34
resemble their models, the models themselves are also	42
changing. Too many good-tasting mimics in a population	50
of untasty models would be unfortunate for both, for if	60
predators were as likely to have a good meal as a bad one,	73
they would begin to dine on mimic and model alike. So it is	86
in the best interest of the model to look as unlike the mimic	99
as possible. Call it anti-mimicry, if you wish.	107

From "Deception: Formula for Survival," page 83

Phrasing

1. ☐ Rarely pauses while reading the text.
2. ☐ Occasionally pauses while reading the text.
3. ☐ Frequently pauses at appropriate points in the text.
4. ☐ Consistently pauses at all appropriate points in the text.

Accuracy and Rate Formula

Use the formula to measure a reader's accuracy and rate while reading aloud.

_____ − _____ = _____
words attempted   number of errors   words correct per minute
in one minute   (wcpm)

2.7

Unit 2 | Survival

Name _____ Date _____

Reading Options

"Living Nightmares"

Complete the fact cards as you read the science feature.

That's Amazing!

An amazing fact about _____

is _____

_____

That's Amazing!

An amazing fact about _____

is _____

_____

That's Amazing!

An amazing fact about _____

is _____

_____

Tell a partner which fact was your favorite and why.

2.8

Unit 2 | Survival

Name _____ Date _____

Respond and Extend

Compare Texts

Fill in the comparison chart to compare the two reading selections.

	"Deception: Formula for Survival"	"Living Nightmares"
Main idea of selection	Some species...	Some species...
Details that support the main idea	1. 2. 3.	1. 2. 3.
Text features		

💬 Use your chart to discuss how the selections develop the same main idea. Work with a partner to combine the information from both texts to summarize how adaptations help animals survive.

Name _____ Date _____

Grammar

Unusual Icefish

Grammar Rules Subject and Object Pronouns

1. Use a **subject pronoun** in place of a **noun** as the subject of a sentence.
2. The subject pronouns are **I**, **you**, **he**, **she**, **it**, **we**, and **they**.
3. Use an **object pronoun** in place of a **noun** after an <u>action verb</u>.
4. Use an **object pronoun** in place of a **noun** after a <u>preposition</u>.
5. The object pronouns are **me**, **you**, **him**, **her**, **it**, **us**, and **them**.

Read the sentence pairs. Write the correct pronoun on each line.

1. The icefish is sometimes called the "white crocodile fish." _____ has a long snout like a crocodile's. _____ probably did not know that, did you?

2. William Detrich has been researching icefish for many years. _____ studies these cold-water creatures and learns about _____.

3. Kristin O'Brien also studies icefish. _____ is worried about these Southern Ocean animals. _____ may be in danger because of climate change.

4. Ms. O'Brien says the ocean is warming. The warmer water is a concern for _____. The icefish and other sea animals may be affected by _____.

Use sentences with subject and object pronouns to talk about the unusual ways some animals stay safe. Ask a partner to identify the pronouns and the nouns that the pronouns refer to.

Name _____ Date _____

Close Reading

from "Living Nightmares," pages 96-97

Analyze the text below with your teacher and make notes.

1. **GHOST SHRIMP** A spookfish isn't the only ghostly sea critter. We spot our next one on a sea anemone. It's hard to see it, because a ghost shrimp's body is mostly clear.

2. The shrimp uses its body as camouflage, so it can blend in wherever it goes. Other critters see only the surface on which the shrimp is standing, so the shrimp remains safely hidden from predators.

3. Being clear only works as long as the ghost shrimp doesn't eat. When the shrimp nibbles algae, its food shows through its transparent body.

4. **GLASS FROG** Another ghostly creature lives in a rain forest; it makes a squeaky "peep" sound. The sound seems like it's coming from a pale, green leaf, but it looks as if there is no critter on the leaf.

5. Suddenly, a bump on the leaf wiggles, and it's a frog. Like the other ghostly creatures you've read about, this frog is a master of disguise. Because it blends in with the leaf, it is almost invisible until it moves. It's not the same color as the leaf, however. Like the shrimp, a glass frog blends in because it has almost no color at all.

Name _____ Date _____

Close Reading

from "Living Nightmares," page 98

Make notes as you read the paragraphs below. Then answer the questions on page 2.13.

1. **ZOMBIE ANT** A line of ants marches through a rain forest. One by one, the ants climb a tree trunk to head up to their warm, dry nest. Suddenly, one ant stumbles out of line, twitches a little, and then drops to the ground. Something is wrong because these ants usually never step out of line.

2. Near the ground, the ant finds a leaf. It crawls under the leaf where it's damp and shady, and then it bites into the leaf. Suddenly, the ant's jaws lock, and it can't let go or even move. The ant hangs from the leaf, slowly dying. This ant is acting odd for a scary reason—because it's a zombie. You can't see it, but a killer now controls the ant.

Name _____ Date _____

Close Reading

from "Living Nightmares" (continued)

Reread and annotate the passage to answer these questions.

Reread paragraph 1.

1. Where do zombie ants live? Highlight text evidence that supports your answer.

2. Underline this sentence: "Suddenly, one ant stumbles out of line, twitches a little, and then drops to the ground." Unpack the meaning of this sentence by breaking it into smaller parts.

3. What is the main idea of paragraph 1? Highlight text evidence to support your answer. Record your main idea in the margin at the end of the paragraph.

Reread paragraph 2.

4. Identify details that tell how the zombie ant suddenly changes. Highlight these details within the text.

5. What is the main idea of paragraph 2? Highlight text evidence to support your answer. Record your main idea in the margin at the end of the paragraph.

6. Visualize the section, and think about the author's word choices. How does the author use a narrative style to help readers visualize the scene?

Name _____ Date _____

Thinking Map

Character

Fill in the character chart as a partner tells you about a time he/she did something important.

Character:	
Motives	**Actions**

Tell a partner about a time you did something important. Have your partner complete the chart to tell what you did and what your motives were. Then discuss what the information in the chart shows about you.

Name _____   Date _____

Grammar

Possessive Nouns: Choose and Write

1. Take turns choosing an unmarked box.
2. Read the **noun** in the box. Write the possessive form on the line.
3. Say the **possessive noun** in a sentence.
4. Have the other players check your work. If they agree that your possessive noun is correct, write your initials in the box.
5. When all the boxes are initialed, count your boxes. The player with the most boxes wins.

Brian _____	mother _____	fathers _____	airplane _____
character _____	children _____	people _____	animals _____
bird _____	partner _____	trees _____	shelter _____
tool _____	voices _____	men _____	night _____
tents _____	friends _____	stomach _____	forest _____

2.15

Unit 2 | Survival

Key Points Reading

"Hatchet"

Listen as your teacher reads. Follow with your finger.

1

Thirteen-year-old Brian Robeson is going to visit his father. He is flying in a small plane when the pilot has a heart attack. Now the plane has crashed, and Brian is all alone in the Canadian north woods.

2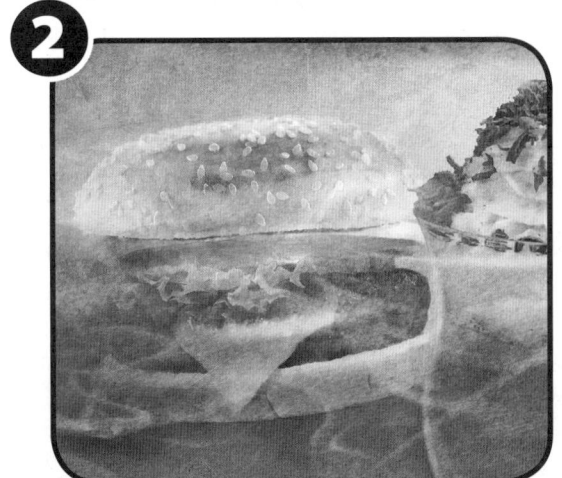

Brian knows people will look for him. He imagines going home and eating a juicy hamburger. Suddenly his hunger is intense, and he tries to think of something else. He remembers a former teacher, Mr. Perpich. Mr. Perpich would have told him to stay positive and motivated.

3

Brian realizes that rescuers may not find him for days. He looks over the items he has to see what might be useful but most seem useless. Then Brian remembers something else Mr. Perpich said: "You are your most valuable asset." This idea is important to Brian. He resolves to help himself survive.

Grammar

Possessive Adjectives and Pronouns: Spin It!

1. Take turns. Spin the spinner. Read the word on the space where you land. Tell if the word is a possessive adjective or a possessive pronoun.
2. Say a sentence with the word.
3. If the other players agree that the sentence is correct, score one point.
4. The first player to get five points is the winner.

Make a Spinner

1. Place one loop of a paper clip over the center of the circle.
2. Push a sharp pencil through the loop and the paper.
3. Spin the paper clip around the pencil.

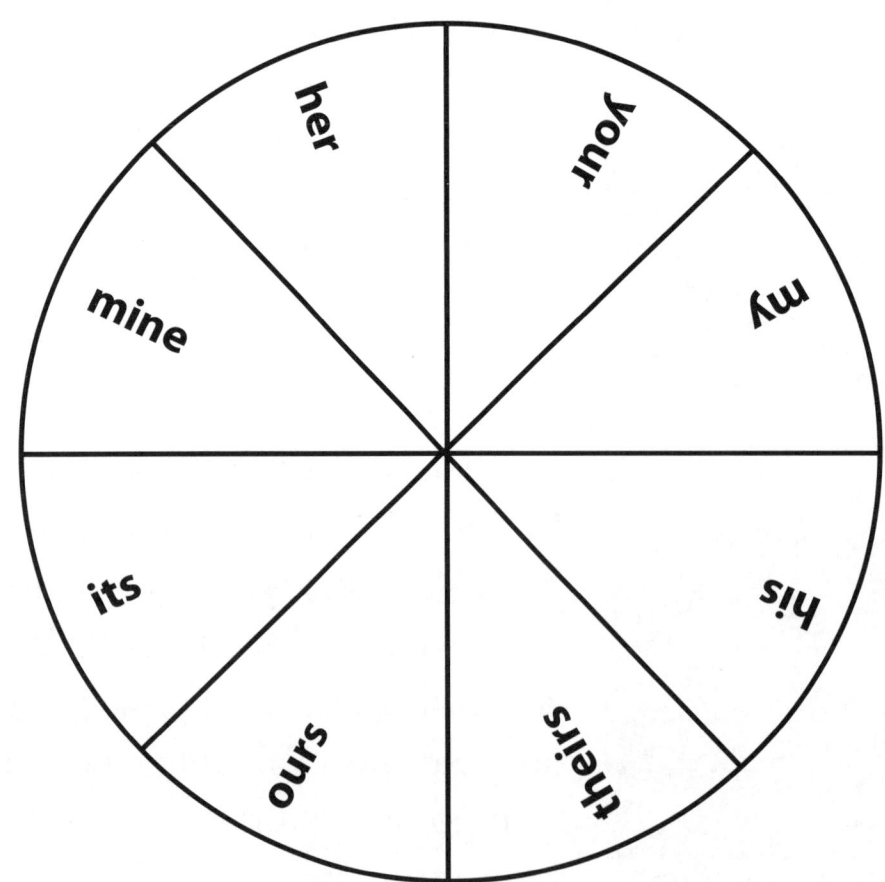

Unit 2 | Survival

Name _____ Date _____

Reread and Retell

Character

Fill in the character chart.

Character: Brian Robeson	
Motives	**Actions**
wants to figure out what is happening	stops panicking and tries to think clearly

 Use your chart to describe Brian's motives and actions. Use what you record to describe Brian to a partner. Explain to your partner what Brian's actions and motivations tell you about his character.

Name _____ Date _____

Fluency

"Hatchet"

Use this passage to practice reading with proper expression.

They would look for him, look for the plane. His	10
father and mother would be frantic. They would tear the	20
world apart to find him. Brian had seen searches on the	31
news, seen movies about lost planes. When a plane went	41
down they mounted extensive searches and almost always	49
they found the plane within a day or two. Pilots all filed flight	62
plans—a detailed plan for where and when they were going	73
to fly, with all the courses explained. They would come, they	84
would look for him. The searchers would get government	93
planes and cover both sides of the flight plan filed by the	105
pilot and search until they found him.	112

From "Hatchet," page 113

Expression
- [ ] 1 Does not read with feeling.
- [ ] 2 Reads with some feeling but does not match content.
- [ ] 3 Reads with appropriate feeling for most content.
- [ ] 4 Reads with appropriate feeling for all content.

Accuracy and Rate Formula
Use the formula to measure a reader's accuracy and rate while reading aloud.

_____ − _____ = _____
words attempted   number of errors   words correct per minute
in one minute   (wcpm)

Name _____ Date _____

Reading Options

"The Girl Who Fell from the Sky"

Complete the prediction chart as you read the personal narrative.

What I know about Juliane	What I think will happen

2.20

Unit 2 | Survival

Name _____   Date _____

Respond and Extend

Compare Choices

Complete the comparison chart with a partner.

	"Hatchet"	"The Girl Who Fell from the Sky"
Person/Character	Brian Robeson	Juliane Koepcke Diller
Problem		
Goal or motive		
Choices made to achieve goal		

Take turns with a partner to complete the chart. Then compare and contrast Brian and Juliane and the choices they made.

Name _____ Date _____

Grammar

Survival Tips

Grammar Rules: Possessive Adjectives and Pronouns

1. A **possessive adjective** comes, before a **noun**.
2. The possessive adjectives are **my**, **your**, **his**, **her**, **its**, **our**, and **their**.
3. A **possessive pronoun** is used in place of one or more **nouns**.
4. The possessive pronouns are **mine**, **yours**, **his**, **hers**, **ours**, and **theirs**.

Write the possessive adjective or possessive pronoun that correctly completes each sentence.

1. If you would like to learn some survival tips, I will share _____ with you.

2. If you are lost, look for a river and stay near _____ banks.

3. When you are hiking, always keep _____ eyes wide open.

4. Smart hikers carry a flashlight and matches in _____ backpacks.

5. I have had my adventures, and you will have _____.

Tell a partner about survival and safety tips you know about. Use sentences with possessive adjectives and possessive pronouns. Ask your partner to identify the possessive adjectives and pronouns. Then exchange roles and repeat.

Name _____ Date _____

Close Reading

from "The Girl Who Fell from the Sky," page 127

Analyze the text below with your teacher and make notes.

1. For someone who has never been in the rain forest, it can seem threatening. Huge trees cast mysterious shadows. Water drips constantly. The rain forest often has a musty smell from the plants that intertwine and ramble, grow and decay.

2. Insects rule the jungle, and I encounter them all: ants, beetles, butterflies, grasshoppers, mosquitoes. A certain type of fly will lay eggs under the skin or in wounds. Stingless wild bees like to cling to hair.

3. Luckily, I'd lived in the jungle long enough as a child to be acquainted with the bugs and other creatures that scurry, rustle, whistle, and snarl. There was almost nothing my parents hadn't taught me about the jungle. I only had to find this knowledge in my concussion-fogged head.

4. Suddenly I'm seized by an intense thirst. Thick drops of water sparkle on the leaves around me, and I lick them up. I walk in small circles around my seat, aware of how quickly you can lose your orientation in the jungle. I memorize the location and markings of one tree to keep my bearings.

Name _____ Date _____

Close Reading

from "The Girl Who Fell from the Sky," page 128

Make notes as you read the paragraphs below. Then answer the questions on page 2.25.

1. I hear the hum of airplane engines overhead. I look up, but the trees are too dense: There's no way I can make myself noticeable here. A feeling of powerlessness overcomes me. I have to get out of the thick of the forest so that rescuers can see me. Soon the engines' hum fades away.

2. I hear the dripping, tinkling, gurgle of water that I hadn't noticed before. Nearby I find a spring, feeding a tiny rivulet. This fills me with hope. Not only have I found water to drink, but I'm convinced that this little stream will lead the way to my rescue.

3. I try to follow the rivulet closely, but there are often tree trunks lying across it, or dense undergrowth blocks my way. Little by little, the rivulet grows wider and turns into a stream, which is partly dry, so that I can easily walk beside the water. Around six o'clock it gets dark, and I look in the streambed for a protected spot where I can spend the night. I eat another candy.

Name _____ Date _____

Close Reading

from "The Girl Who Fell from the Sky" (continued)

Reread and annotate the passage to answer these questions.

Reread paragraph 1.

1. Diller writes: "There's no way I can make myself noticeable here." Highlight text evidence that supports Diller's claim, and explain what she means.

Reread paragraph 2.

2. Why is the tiny rivulet of water so important to Diller? Highlight text evidence that supports your answer.

Reread paragraph 3.

3. Underline: "Little by little, the rivulet grows wider and turns into a stream, which is partly dry, so that I can easily walk beside the water." Unpack the meaning of this sentence. Why is being able to walk beside the water such a good thing for Diller?

4. What are two things Diller does to keep herself safe and strong when it starts to get dark? Highlight text evidence that supports your answer.

Name _____   Date _____

Writing Project

Organization

Writing is organized when it is easy to follow. All the ideas make sense together and flow from one idea to the next in an order that fits the writer's audience and purpose.

	Is the expository report organized?	Does the writing flow?
4 Wow!	❏ The writing is clearly organized around a main idea and supporting details. The organization fits the purpose of an expository report.	❏ The ideas flow smoothly and logically. The writer used transition words to connect the ideas.
3 Ahh.	❏ The writing is organized around a main idea and supporting details, but a few details are out of place.	❏ Most ideas flow logically. The writer used some transition words, but there are a few unconnected ideas.
2 Hmm.	❏ The writing has a main idea and supporting details, but many details are out of place.	❏ The order of ideas makes some sense. The writing jumps from one idea to another, but I can follow what it says.
1 Huh?	❏ The writing is not organized. The writer may have forgotten to use a main idea chart to plan.	❏ I can't follow the writer's ideas. The writing jumps around too much.

Name _____ Date _____

Writing Project

Main Idea Chart

Complete the main idea chart for your expository report.

Main idea

Detail 1	Detail 2

Name _____ Date _____

Writing Project

Revise

Use revision marks to make changes to these paragraphs. Look for:

- a logical organization
- transition words
- details and examples that support the main idea

Revision Marks	
∧	Add
℘	Take out
◯⌒∧	Move to here
/	Make lowercase

Sea Butterflies

Even the smallest creatures contribute to the ecosystem and help larger animals survive. Sea butterflies are tiny snails that are about the size of a pea and live in the ocean. They use their wing-like fins to swim in large groups on ocean currents.

Polar bears eat ringed seals. Ringed seals got their name from the circular patterns on their backs. Sea butterflies eat plankton. One of Earth's smallest predators, the sea butterfly, is linked to one of Earth's largest predators, the polar bear. Ringed seals eat sea butterflies.

Rewrite your revised paragraph on the lines.

_____
_____
_____
_____

Name _____ Date _____

Writing Project

Edit and Proofread

Use revision marks to edit and proofread these paragraphs. Look for:

- correct use of subject, object, and possessive pronouns
- correct use of possessive adjectives
- correct use of commas with introductory words or phrases

Revision Marks	
∧	Add
℘	Take out
∧̸	Insert comma

Hiding in Plain Sight

Insects often use clever adaptations to avoid predators. Mimicry is one way we do this. For example some butterflies resemble other bad-tasting butterflies so birds will not want to eat it. The harmless viceroy butterfly looks very similar to the poisonous, unpleasant-tasting monarch butterfly. As a result of this birds leave the viceroy alone. The first scientist to describe this kind of mimicry was Henry Walter Bates. Him was an English naturalist in the 1800s.

Camouflage is another way that insects use theirs appearance to fool predators. The thorn bug is a good example. With a body that looks like a thorn it can rest on a branch and blend into their surroundings. Clever adaptations like this are everywhere in nature. Insects have theirs. What are your?

Name _____   Date _____

Unit Concept Map

Digging Up the Past

Make a concept map with the answers to the Big Question:
How can we bring the past to life?

How can we bring the past to life?		
What I <u>know</u> already	What I <u>want</u> to know	What I <u>learned</u>
People study Egyptian pyramids and mummies.	How can mummies help us learn about the past?	

Name _____ Date _____

Thinking Map
Chronological Order

Fill in the double time line below.

Historical events

More recent events

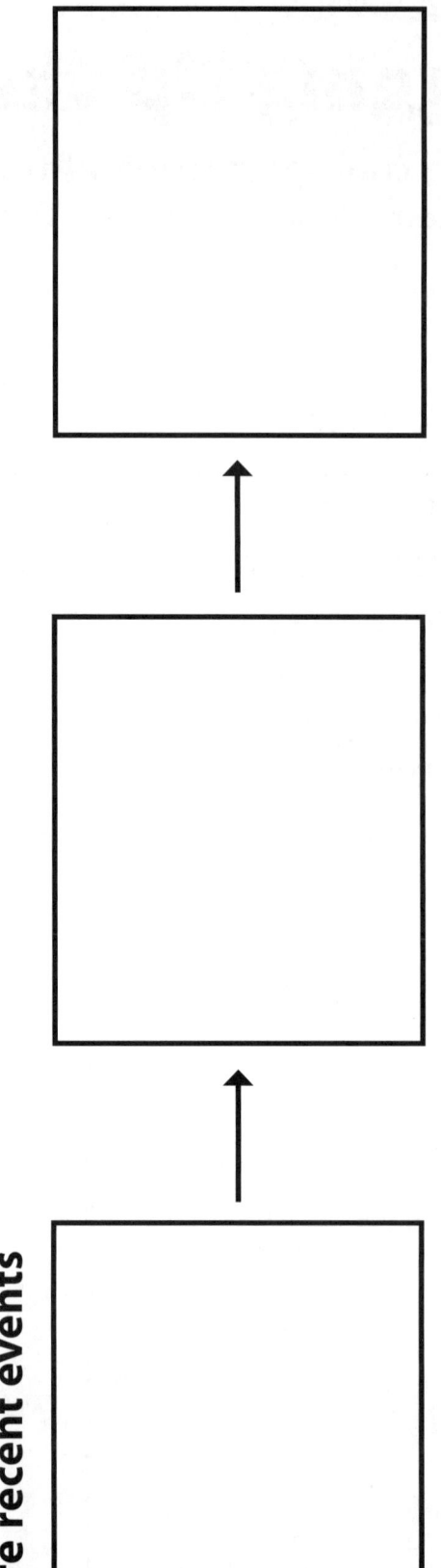

Use your double time line to record events from your family's past and from present-day activities.

© Cengage Learning, Inc.

3.2   Unit 3 | Digging Up the Past

Name _____ Date _____

Grammar

Present Progressive Verbs

Rewrite each verb in the present progressive form.

1. The archaeologists _____ in the sand. (dig)

2. The wind _____ sand into their eyes. (blow)

3. They _____ about the past. (learn)

4. That woman _____ a small statue. (clean)

5. I _____ pictures of the wall. (take)

6. The scientists _____ about the artifact. (talk)

Rewrite sentences 5 and 6 as negative sentences.

_____

_____

_____

_____

Take turns with a partner to describe what is happening now in the classroom. Use the present progressive tense.

Key Points Reading

"Valley of the Kings"

Listen as your teacher reads. Follow with your finger.

In 1825, James Burton explored the first few rooms of a tomb in the Valley of the Kings in Egypt. He drew a sketch of what he saw. The tomb, later named KV 5, was forgotten for more than 150 years. In 1989, Dr. Kent Weeks began a mapping project in the Valley of the Kings. He and his team found KV 5 and went inside.

Dr. Weeks and his team explored the tomb. They crawled through the debris into the large hall Burton had sketched. At the back of the hall was a doorway. Beyond this doorway was a long corridor with many more doorways. A tall statue of the god Osiris stood at the end of the hallway. More corridors went off to the sides.

Carvings on the walls show that KV 5 is the tomb of several sons of Ramses II. Ramses II was a powerful pharaoh. He had a long and successful rule. He also had many children. Dr. Weeks estimates that up to 20 sons are buried in KV 5. Dr. Weeks and his team continue to excavate KV 5. It is the largest tomb ever found. It has over 110 chambers.

Name _____ Date _____

Grammar

Spin a Tense

Directions:

1. Play with a partner. Take turns.
2. Spin the paper clip. Read the **verb**.
3. Write a sentence using the **past progressive** or **future progressive** form of the verb.
4. If your partner agrees that you have formed the verb correctly and that you have spelled the main verb correctly, score one point.
5. Give your partner a turn.
6. After all the verbs have been used once, count your points. The player with the most points wins.

Make a Spinner

1. Place one loop of a paper clip over the center of the circle.
2. Push a sharp pencil through the loop and the paper.
3. Spin the paper clip around the pencil.

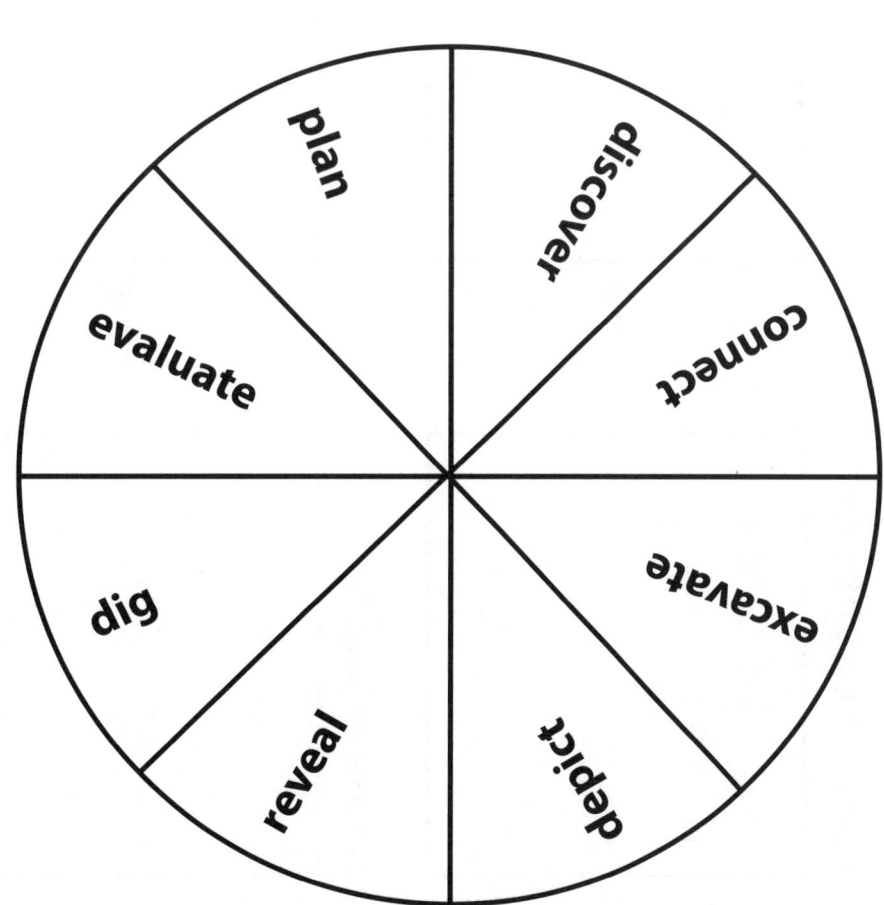

3.5

Unit 3 | Digging Up the Past

Name _____ Date _____

Reread and Retell
"Valley of the Kings"

Fill in the double time line below.

Ancient Egyptians

| 1303 B.C.E.: Ramses II is born. | → | | → | |

Archaeologists

| 1825 C.E.: Burton sketches chambers in a small tomb. | → | | → | |

Use your double time line to record events from the text. Summarize the first time line for a partner. Your partner summarizes the second time line for you. Discuss how the events are related.

© Cengage Learning, Inc.

3.6   Unit 3 | Digging Up the Past

Name _____ Date _____

Fluency

"Valley of the Kings"

Use this passage to practice reading with proper phrasing.

"Look," Ahmed said. He was pointing to a gap	9
in the wall of debris that lay ahead.	17
I shone my flashlight into the gap. There was nothing but blackness.	29
Strange, I thought. The light should reflect off a wall.	39
Crawling forward, we found the corridor. It was about nine feet wide	51
and continued a hundred feet into the hillside.	59
There was one door on the left, another on the right, then two more, then four.	75
We counted doors as we crawled forward: 10, 12, 16, 18.	86
Other tomb corridors in the Valley of the Kings	95
have at most one or two doorways cut into their walls.	106
I had never seen a corridor like this one in any Egyptian tomb.	119

From "Valley of the Kings," page 156

Phrasing

1. ☐ Rarely pauses while reading the text.
2. ☐ Occasionally pauses while reading the text.
3. ☐ Frequently pauses at appropriate points in the text.
4. ☐ Consistently pauses at all appropriate points in the text.

Accuracy and Rate Formula

Use the formula to measure a reader's accuracy and rate while reading aloud.

_____ − _____ = _____
words attempted   number of errors   words correct per minute
in one minute   (wcpm)

3.7   Unit 3 | Digging Up the Past

Name _____   Date _____

Reading Options

"Animals Everlasting"

Complete the K-W-L-Q chart as you read the magazine article.

K What I know	W What I want to learn	L What I learned	Q Questions I still have

Share your questions with a partner. Try to answer the questions together.

Name _____ Date _____

Respond and Extend

Compare Information

Fill in the comparison chart below.

	"Valley of the Kings"	"Animals Everlasting"
Topic		An Egyptologist studies animal mummies.
Text	details about the structure, art, remains, and chambers in the tomb	
Main ideas		
Text features		

Talk with a partner. Discuss how information from both texts adds to your knowledge of ancient Egypt and brings the past to life.

3.9

Unit 3 | Digging Up the Past

Name _____ Date _____

Grammar

Treasure in the Trash

Grammar Rules Progressive Tenses

1. A **present progressive verb** tells about an action as it is happening. It uses the helping verb **am**, **is**, or **are**.
2. A **past progressive verb** tells about an action that was happening over a period of time in the past. It uses the helping verb **was** or **were**.
3. A **future progressive verb** tells about an action that will be happening over a period of time in the future. It uses the helping verbs **will be**.

Circle the verbs in the progressive tense. Underline the helping verbs.

Archaeologists constantly are exploring ways to learn how people lived in the past. Often, they study garbage. As researchers sift through the debris left behind in trash heaps, they are finding tools, pottery shards, and even bones. When people long ago threw away their trash, they were not thinking about the future. But now, these artifacts are giving new insights into the past. Archaeologists will be studying them for years to come.

Write two new sentences with a helping verb and a verb in the progressive tense. Ask a partner to read your sentences and identify which progressive tenses you used.

Name _____ Date _____

Close Reading

from "Animals Everlasting," pages 167–168

Analyze the text below with your teacher and make notes.

1. For many decades, archaeologists and treasure seekers led expeditions through the Egyptian desert. Their quest was to find royal tombs and splendid gold and painted masks and coffins. These would be sent to adorn the estates and museums of Europe and America. Lying among the ancient artifacts lay many thousands of mummified animals that turned up at sacred sites throughout Egypt. To those early explorers, the carefully preserved remains were just things to be cleared away to get at the good stuff. Few people studied them, and their importance was generally unrecognized.

2. In the past century, archaeology has become less of a trophy hunt and more of a science. Excavators now realize that much of their sites' wealth lies in the multitude of details about ordinary folks. Archaeologists want to know what they did, what they thought, how they prayed. Animal mummies are a big part of that pay dirt.

3.11   Unit 3 | Digging Up the Past

Name _____   Date _____

Close Reading

from "Animals Everlasting," pages 168–169

Make notes as you read the paragraphs below. Then answer the questions on page 3.13.

1. As a professor at the American University in Cairo, she [Salima Ikram] adopted the Egyptian Museum's languishing collection of animal mummies as a research project. She spent time taking precise measurements, peering beneath linen bandages with x-rays, and cataloging her findings. Then she created a gallery for the collection. The result was a bridge between people today and those of long ago. "You look at these animals, and suddenly you say, Oh, King So-and-So had a pet. I have a pet. And instead of being at a distance of 5,000-plus years, the ancient Egyptians become people."

2. Today the animal mummies are one of the most popular exhibits in the whole treasure-filled museum. Visitors of all ages, Egyptians and foreigners, press in shoulder to shoulder to get a look. Behind glass panels lie cats wrapped in strips of linen that form diamonds, stripes, squares, and crisscrosses. Shrews in boxes of carved limestone. Rams covered with gilded and beaded casings. A gazelle wrapped in a tattered mat of papyrus, so thoroughly flattened by mummification that Ikram named it Roadkill.

Name _____ Date _____

Close Reading

from "Animals Everlasting" (continued)

Reread and annotate the passage to answer these questions.

Reread paragraph 1.

1. Underline, look up, and write the meaning of the adjective *languishing* in the margin. Discuss with a partner. Do you think Ikram will let the mummies continue to languish? Highlight text evidence to support your answer.

2. How does Ikram feel about the animal mummies? How do you know? Highlight text evidence that supports your answer.

3. The author says Ikram created "a bridge between people today and those of long ago." Highlight text evidence that supports this claim, and explain what the author means.

Reread paragraph 2.

4. How were animal mummies created? Highlight text evidence. What do the details tell you about the people who preserved the animals?

5. Think about the main ideas of the two paragraphs. Write a summary sentence in the margin that explains why Ikram's work with the museum exhibit is important.

3.13 Unit 3 | Digging Up the Past

Name _____ Date _____

Thinking Map

Plot

Fill in the plot diagram below.

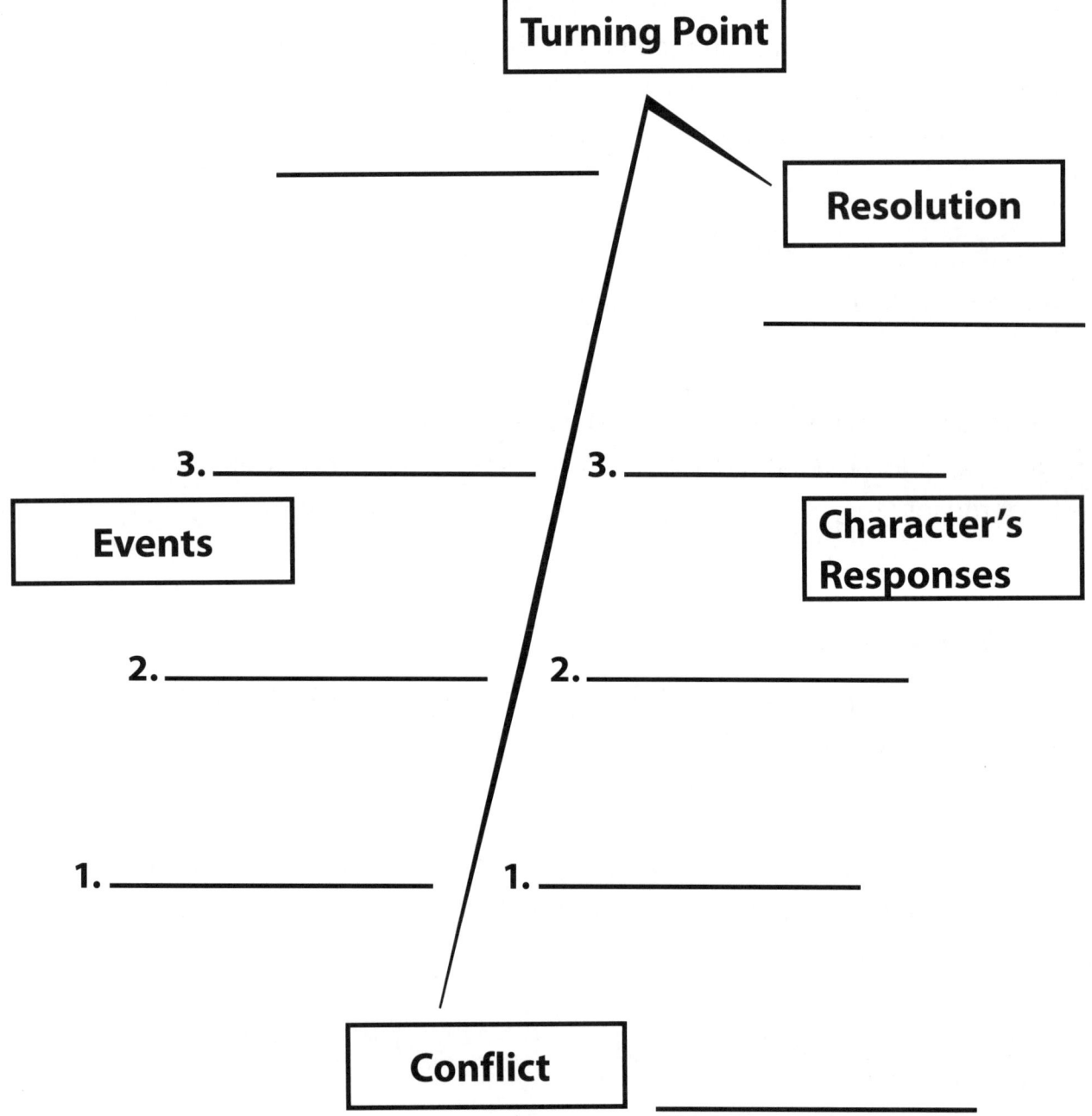

Identify the conflict in a story you have read, such as "The Spark of Determination." Then complete the plot diagram to tell how the character responds to story events to move the plot to a resolution.

3.14 Unit 3 | Digging Up the Past

Grammar

Contraction Match

Directions:

1. Play with a partner.
2. Make word cards, and place them face down on a playing surface.
3. Take turns turning over cards and trying to match each **contraction** to the words it stands for.
4. The player with the most matches is the winner.

I will	he is	you're	were not
aren't	they will	she's	I am
weren't	won't	I'll	we are
she is	he's	we're	they'll
I'm	you are	will not	are not

Unit 3 | Digging Up the Past

Key Points Reading

"Ahmes's Journal"

Listen as your teacher reads. Follow with your finger.

1

First month of the planting season: Ahmes helps in his father's workshop, making vases, plates, and jewelry. He makes a friend named Nebamun. Nebamun is a noble, so he is allowed to go to school. Ahmes would love to go to school to become a scribe.

2

Second month of the planting season: Ahmes's brother is not good at crafts, so the family sends him away to find other work. This makes it even more important for Ahmes to continue helping his father. But he secretly practices writing hieroglyphics. Ahmes is surprised and excited when he is allowed to go to school to become a scribe.

3

First month of the harvesting season: Ahmes goes to school with Nebamun and does well there. Ahmes feels lucky that he is given the opportunity to do what he loves.

Name _____ Date _____

Grammar

Spin a Tense

Directions:

1. Play with a partner. Take turns.
2. Write **modals** *can, could, may, might, must,* and *should,* each on a separate card. Place the cards face down.
3. Player 1 picks a card and spins the spinner. He or she then uses the **modal** on the card and the **main verb** on which the spinner lands to write a sentence.
4. If both players agree that Player 1 has used the verbs correctly, he or she scores a point.
5. Then Player 2 takes a turn.
6. When you run out of modals, mix up the cards, turn them over, and continue playing.
7. After all the verbs on the wheel have been used once, count your points. The player with the most points is the winner.

Make a Spinner

1. Place one loop of a paper clip over the center of the circle.
2. Push a sharp pencil through the loop and the paper.
3. Spin the paper clip around the pencil.

Spinner verbs: turn, plant, command, study, plunder, consider, punish, find

Unit 3 | Digging Up the Past

Name _____   Date _____

Vocabulary

Vocabulary Bingo

Play Bingo using the Key Words from this unit.

3.18

Unit 3 | Digging Up the Past

Name _____ Date _____

Reread and Retell

"Ahmes's Journal"

Fill in the plot diagram below.

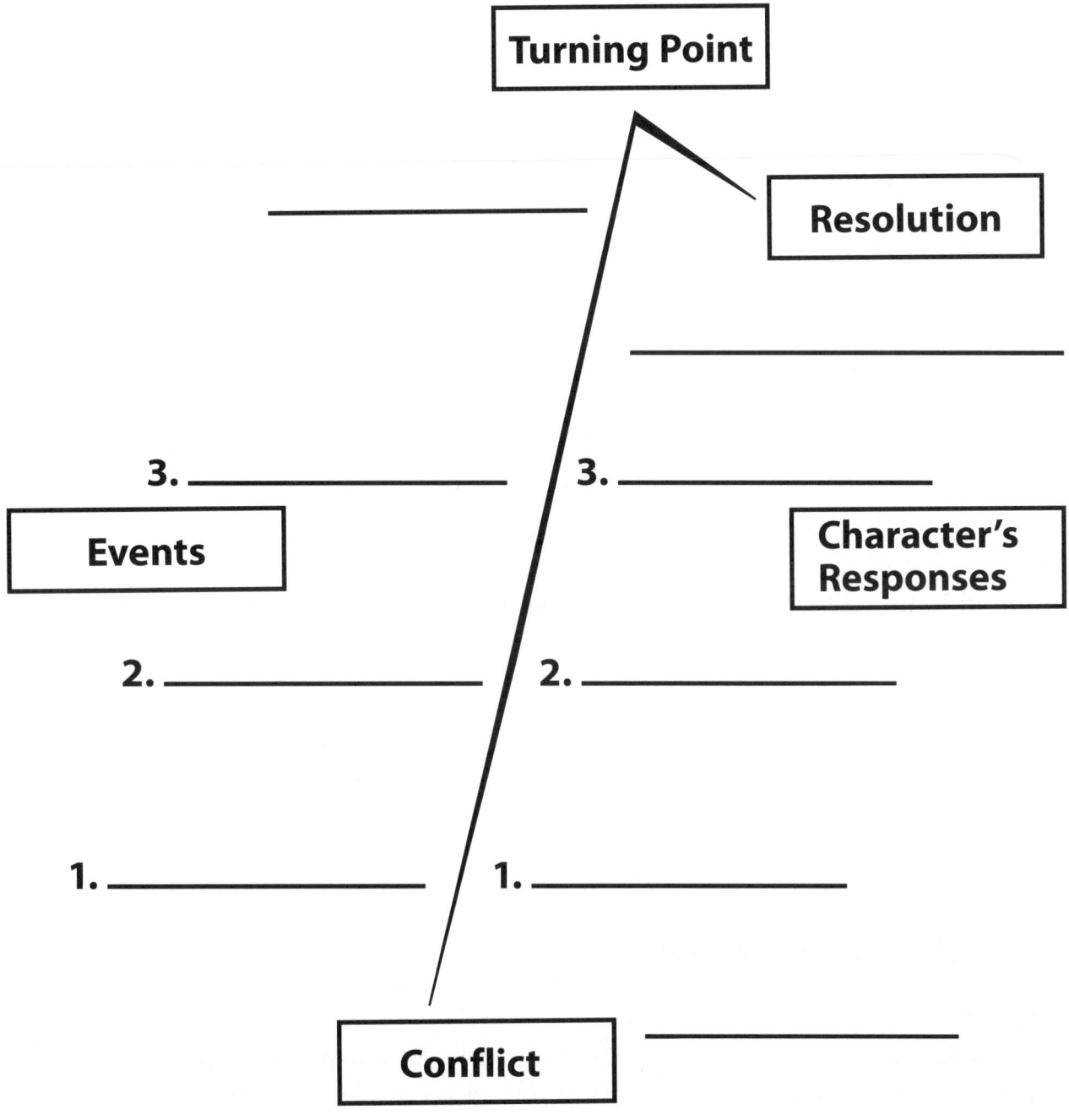

 Complete the plot diagram, and use it to retell "Ahmes's Journal" to a partner.

3.19

Unit 3 | Digging Up the Past

Fluency

"Ahmes's Journal"

Use this passage to practice reading with proper expression.

I still can't believe what happened at the banquet. I didn't know	12
my father and Nebamun's father had a surprise for me. When the banquet	25
was almost over, Nebamun's father called my name and asked me, in front	38
of everyone, math problems and questions about our history. I was able to	51
answer all of them, and I didn't hesitate when he asked me to read a papyrus	67
with hieroglyphics he had written. It wasn't difficult; it was an account of	80
activities in his household. I read it fluently, and he asked whether I could	94
write something like that. The question made me uncomfortable because	104
I still don't know some things needed to do this hard work. I was silent for	120
a moment, and I looked to the ground. I felt the weight of the world on my	137
shoulders.	138

From "Ahmes's Journal," page 194

Expression
1. ☐ Does not read with feeling.
2. ☐ Reads with some feeling, but does not match content.
3. ☐ Reads with appropriate feeling for most content.
4. ☐ Reads with appropriate feeling for all content.

Accuracy and Rate Formula
Use the formula to measure a reader's accuracy and rate while reading aloud.

_____ − _____ = _____
words attempted   number of errors   words correct per minute
in one minute   (wcpm)

Name _____   Date _____

Reading Options

"The Golden Goblet"

Complete the reflection journal as you read the historical fiction.

Page	My question	The answer

▶ Talk with a partner about one of your questions and how you found the answer.

Name _____ Date _____

Respond and Extend

Compare Details

Fill in the comparison chart below.

	"Ahmes's Journal"	"The Golden Goblet"
Genre		Historical fiction
Narrator's point of view	First person: Ahmes writes about his own thoughts and feelings.	
Historical facts		
Fictional details		
Theme		

 Take turns with a partner. Discuss information from both texts. Tell how you learned about the past.

3.22

Unit 3 | Digging Up the Past

Name _____ Date _____

Grammar

Ahmes's Future as a Scribe

Grammar Rules Modals

1. Use **can** to tell what someone or something is able to do.
2. Use **could, may,** or **might** to tell what is possible or permitted.
3. Use **should** to tell what is good for someone to do.
4. Use **must** to tell what somebody has to do or needs to do.
5. Use **would** to tell that somebody is willing to do something.

Read each sentence. Replace the part of the sentence in parentheses with a modal.

1. "I (am able to) help in Father's workshop," Ahmes said.
   "I _____can_____ help in Father's workshop," Ahmes said.

2. His brother said, "We (it is good for us to) stay with the family business."
   His brother said, "We _____ stay with the family business."

3. Ahmes knew he (needed to) talk with his father about his future.
   Ahmes knew he _____ talk with his father about his future.

4. Nebamun's father said he (was willing to) help Ahmes become a scribe.
   "Nebamun's father said he _____ help Ahmes become a scribe.

5. "You (are permitted to) study hieroglypics," Father said.
   "You _____ study hieroglyphics," Father said.

🗨 **Continue with a partner. Take turns using sentences with modals.**

Close Reading

from "The Golden Goblet," page 203

Analyze the text below with your teacher and make notes.

1. As Ranofer looked into their quiet golden faces the stealthy sounds of plundering in the next room became horrible to him. For the first time he fully understood this crime.

2. He straightened, all his fear gone and in its place hot fury. Those merciless and wicked ones!—to break into this sacred place and steal the treasures meant to comfort this old couple through their Three Thousand Years! Whether rich gold or worn-out sandals, these things belonged to them, no living human had a right to set foot in this chamber, not even the son of Thutra, who meant no harm. Almost, he could hear the helpless fluttering of these Old Ones' frightened *bas*. So strong was the sensation that he dropped to his knees in profound apology for his own intrusion. As he did so he saw something else, a stack of wine jars just beyond one of the coffins. They were capped with linen and sealed with clay, and pressed into the clay was a mark as well known to Ranofer as it was to everyone else in Egypt. It was the personal seal of the great noble, Huaa, only two years dead, the beloved father of Queen Tiy.

Name _____ Date _____

Close Reading

from "The Golden Goblet," page 205

Make notes as you read the paragraphs below. Then answer the questions on page 3.26.

1   *"Ast!"* came Wenamon's hiss. "I told you we were not alone!"

2   "We will be soon," Gebu answered in tones that turned Ranofer cold. He could see their two shadows on the wall, black and clear-cut: Gebu's bulky one, Wenamon's thin and vulture-shaped, behind it. The shadows moved, rippled in deadly silence along the wall, leaped crazily to the rough ceiling and down again as the two began methodically to search the room. The dancing black shapes advanced relentlessly toward the coffins, looming huge as giants as they came nearer. Ranofer's hand groped out blindly and closed on a small heavy object that felt like a jewel box. At that instant Gebu's rage-distorted face was thrust over the coffin.

3   Ranofer lunged to his feet and hurled the box with all his strength.

Name _____ Date _____

Close Reading

from "The Golden Goblet" (continued)

Reread and annotate the passage to answer these questions.

Reread paragraph 1.

1. Which characters are in this passage of the story? Highlight text evidence.

2. How does Wenamon feel? Highlight text evidence that supports your claim.

Reread paragraph 2.

3. The author says seeing Wenamon and Gebu "turned Ranofer cold," which means "scared Ranofer." How does the author describe Wenamon and Gebu to show that they are scary to Ranofer? Highlight text evidence.

Reread paragraph 3.

4. Underline and unpack the meaning of the last sentence of the passage. Rephrase the last sentence in your own words, and annotate the text.

5. Throughout the passages, Ranofer is scared of the robbers. How does he find the courage to throw a box at them? Use text evidence.

Name _____ Date _____

Writing Project

Ideas

Writing is well-developed when the message is clear and interesting to the reader. It is supported by details that show the writer knows the topic well.

	Is the report's central idea clear and focused?	Do the details show that the writer knows the topic?
4 Wow!	❏ The central idea is clear and focused. ❏ The writing is interesting and includes signal words to link ideas.	❏ All the facts and details tell about the topic and support the central idea. ❏ The writer knows the topic well.
3 Ahh.	❏ The central idea is fairly clear and focused. ❏ Most of the writing is interesting. It includes some signal words that link ideas.	❏ Most of the facts and details tell about the topic and support the central idea. ❏ The writer knows the topic fairly well.
2 Hmm.	❏ The central idea is not very clear or focused. ❏ Some of the writing holds my attention, but some is hard to follow. Some ideas feel unconnected.	❏ Some of the facts and details do not tell about the topic or support the central idea. ❏ The writer doesn't know the topic well.
1 Huh?	❏ The central idea is difficult to understand. ❏ The writing is confusing and doesn't hold my attention. Ideas are unconnected.	❏ Many facts or details are not about the topic or central idea. ❏ The writer does not seem to know about the topic.

Name _____ Date _____

Writing Project

Brainstorm Your Topic

Use the idea web to brainstorm possible topics for your research report. After you complete it, circle the topic that is most interesting to you.

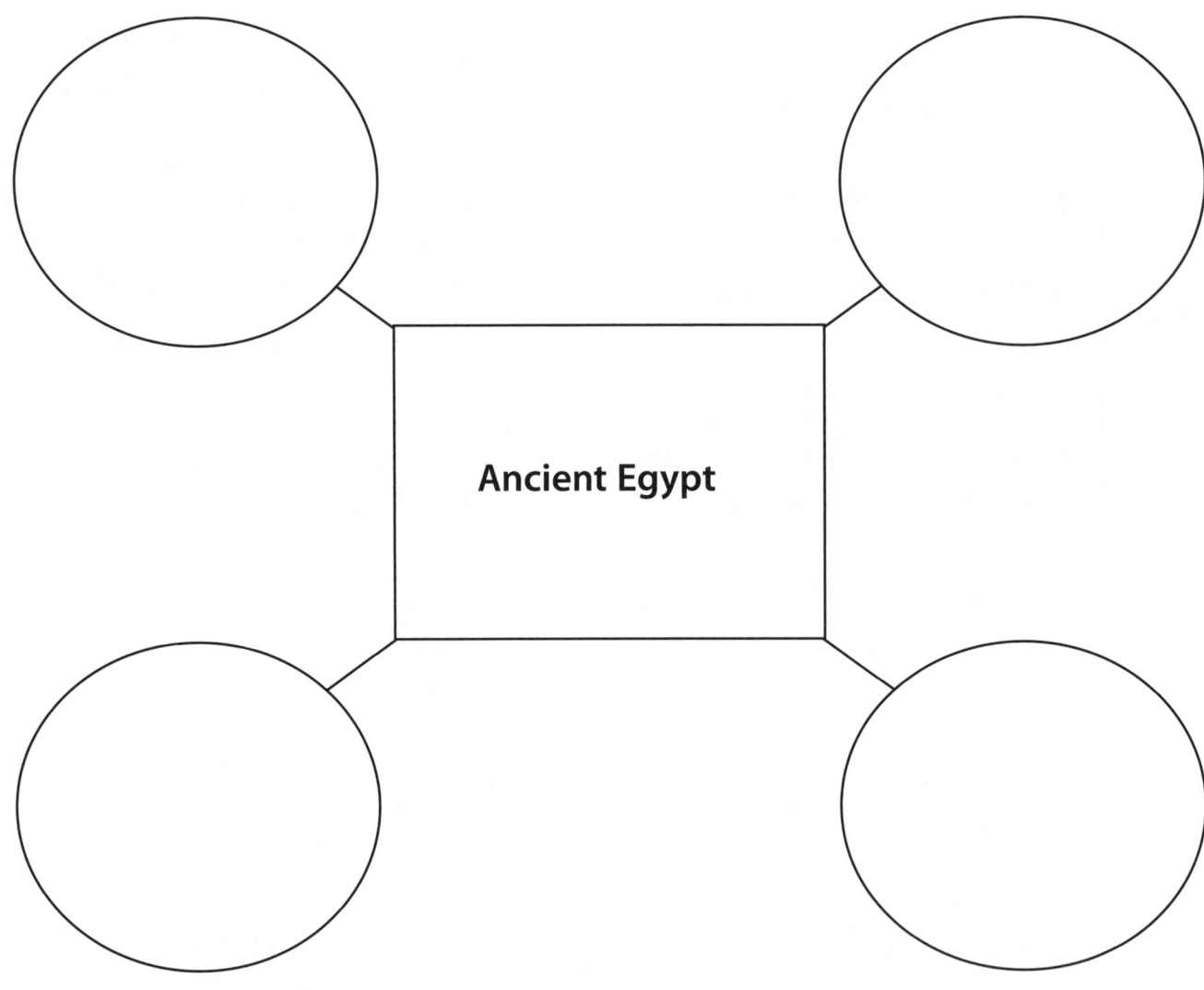

3.28

Unit 3 | Digging Up the Past

Name _____ Date _____

Writing Project

Source Cards

Create a source card for each source you use.

Title/Media Type:	Card Number:
Author/Name of Site:	
Publisher/Site Sponsor and Date:	
URL, if from the Internet:	

Title/Media Type:	Card Number:
Author/Name of Site:	
Publisher/Site Sponsor and Date:	
URL, if from the Internet:	

Unit 3 | Digging Up the Past

Name _____ Date _____

Writing Project

Outline

Use your note cards to create an outline. Use Roman numerals for main ideas. Use capital letters for supporting points. Use Arabic numbers (1., 2., 3.) for details.

I. _____
_____
_____
_____

II. _____
_____
_____
_____
_____

III. _____
_____
_____
_____

IV. _____
_____
_____
_____
_____

Name _____   Date _____

Writing Project

Revise

Use revision marks to make changes to this paragraph. Look for:

- a logical grouping of ideas, facts, and events
- relevant supporting details and examples
- signal words and phrases that link ideas

Revision Marks	
∧	Add
℘	Take out
∧̓	Insert comma
⌒∧	Move to here
/	Make lowercase

Dr. Schaden's Find

Dr. Otto Schaden was working quietly at a little-known tomb. Most archeologists dream of unearthing a find as important as the discovery of King Tut's tomb in 1922. So did Dr. Schaden. He only had a few more hours to work. The tomb was in the Valley of the Kings. Dr. Schaden was born in 1971. It was the end of the digging season. Then he noticed that some rocks were blocking the entrance to a shaft. He was forced to stop for the year.

Rewrite your revised paragraph on the lines.

_____
_____
_____
_____
_____
_____

Writing Project

Edit and Proofread

Use revision marks to edit and proofread these paragraphs. Look for:

- correct spelling of words with suffixes
- correct use of modals
- correct punctuation of quotations

Revision Marks	
∧	Add
✐	Take out
ʽʼ	Insert quotation marks
∩	Change order

Dr. Schaden's Find (continued)

When the workors opened the tomb on March 5, 2006, "a rush of warm air and a smell of myrrh was emitted, Dr. Schaden said in his book. Seven coffins and 28 storage jars were uncovered. People were excited. They may not imagine what wonderfull things they were about to learn from the artifacts in the tomb.

When the coffins were opened, however, there were no mummies. Instead the coffins were filled with supplies such as embalming salt, linens, and resin. When describing the contents of a baby-size coffin, Dr. Schaden said, It was probably a funeral figurine—a mummiform figure that serves as a possible substitute for the deceased".

Even though Dr. Schaden did not discover any mummies, his work is considered a great achievmant.

Name _____ Date _____

Unit Concept Map

Our Diverse Earth

Make a concept map with the answers to the Big Question:
Why is diversity important?

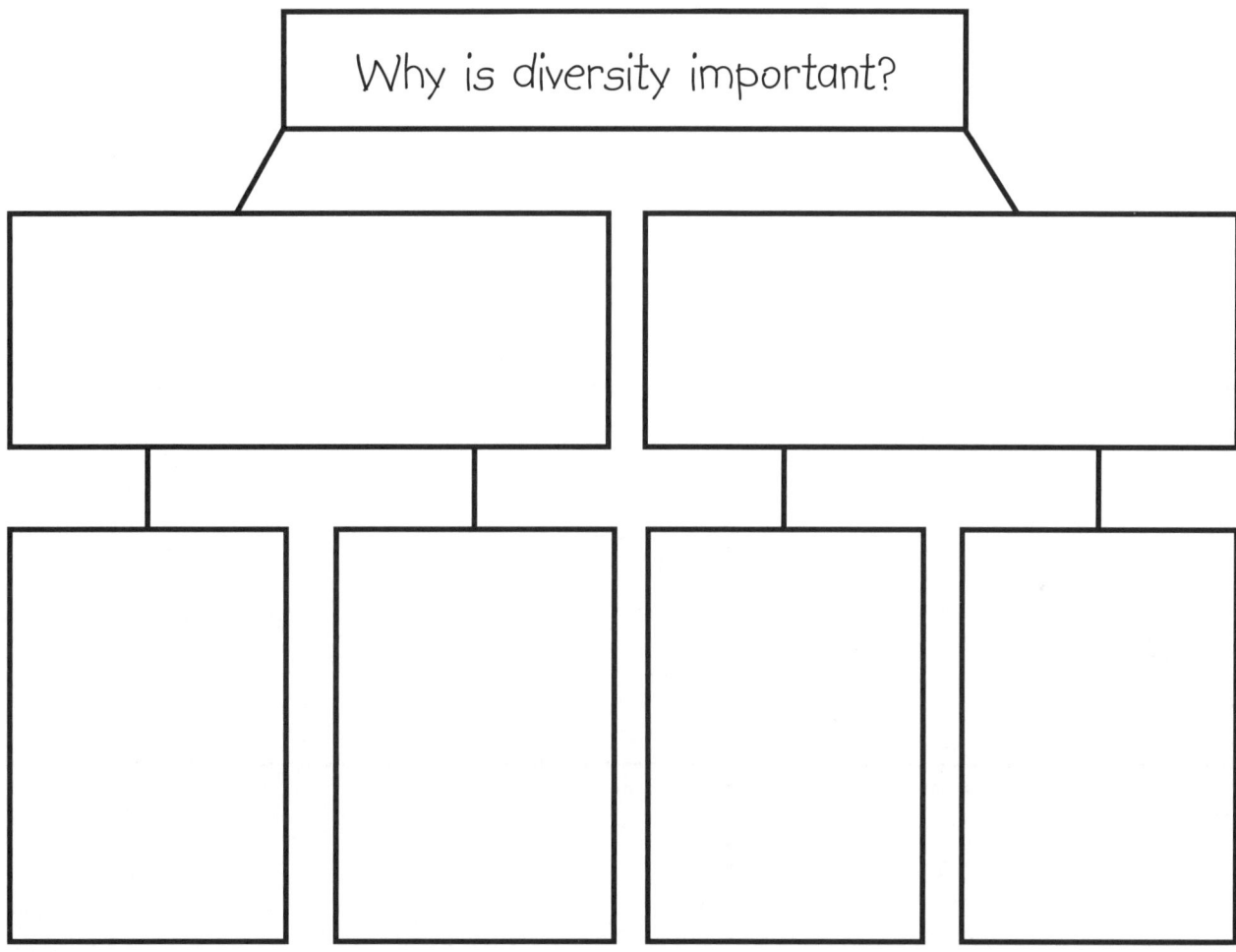

4.1   Unit 4 | Our Diverse Earth

Name _____ Date _____

Thinking Map

Author's Viewpoint

Use the viewpoint chart to record your ideas and form an argument.

Text evidence	Author's viewpoint

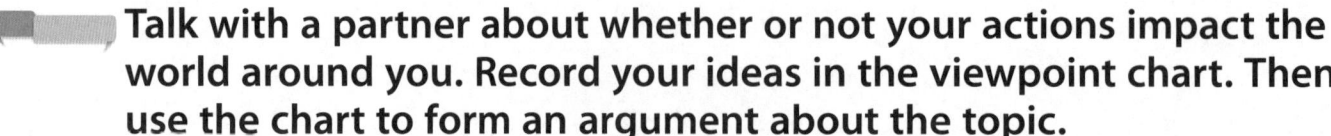 **Talk with a partner** about whether or not your actions impact the world around you. Record your ideas in the viewpoint chart. Then use the chart to form an argument about the topic.

4.2   Unit 4 | Our Diverse Earth

Name _____ Date _____

Grammar

Adjective Tic-Tac-Toe

1. Play with a partner. Player 1 is "X" and Player 2 is "O."

2. Player 1 chooses a **noun** and says a sentence that uses the noun with an **adjective**.

3. Player 2 names the adjective. If Player 2 is correct, he or she writes "O" in the square. If Player 2 is incorrect, Player 1 writes "X" in the square.

4. Player 2 chooses a **noun** and says a sentence that uses the noun with an **adjective** for Player 1 to name.

5. Take turns choosing words and saying sentences.

6. The first player to get three Xs or Os in a row wins.

river	trees	boats
park	habitat	laws
species	pollution	wolves

4.3

Unit 4 | Our Diverse Earth

Name _____   Date _____

Key Points Reading

"A Natural Balance"

Listen as your teacher reads. Follow with your finger.

Our Effect on the Environment

Everything you do affects the environment. Your actions affect living things and nonliving things, such as air and water. Some actions help animal and plant populations thrive. But other actions harm the environment. For example, water pollution can harm or kill plants and animals that live in the water.

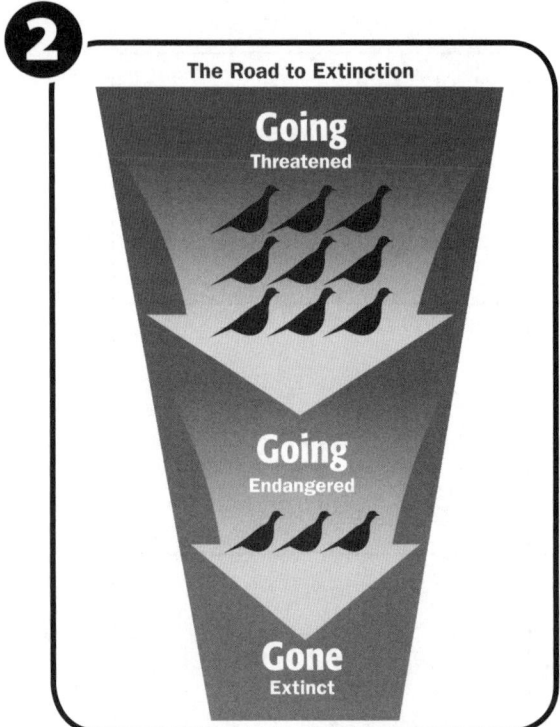

Are We Solving the Problem?

When the population of a species gets too small, it is endangered. If an endangered species does not get help, it could become extinct.

To help protect endangered species, the U.S. government passed the Endangered Species Act in 1973. This policy protects endangered species and where they live.

Name _____ Date _____

Key Points Reading

"A Natural Balance" (continued)

A Balancing Act

Sometimes helping a species interferes with human lives. The gray wolf is one example. To help this endangered animal, scientists brought 31 wolves from Canada to Yellowstone National Park. The wolves hunted elk, deer, and other wild animals. Their numbers grew to 400–450 wolves.

The growing wolf population caused problems for many ranchers. Some wolves attacked cattle and other farm animals. Ranchers are in the business of raising animals. They know that wolves must be protected, but they also want to protect their animals. To solve the problem, it is important to find a balance that protects people and animals.

Name _____ Date _____

Grammar

Adverb Spinner

1. Play with a partner. Take turns spinning the spinner. Follow the directions in the space you land on. Use the **adverb** in a sentence.

2. If your partner agrees that the sentence is correct, give yourself a point.

3. Play until both of you have spun eight times. Who has more points?

Make a Spinner

1. Place one loop of a paper clip over the center of the circle.
2. Push a sharp pencil through the loop and the paper.
3. Spin the paper clip around the pencil.

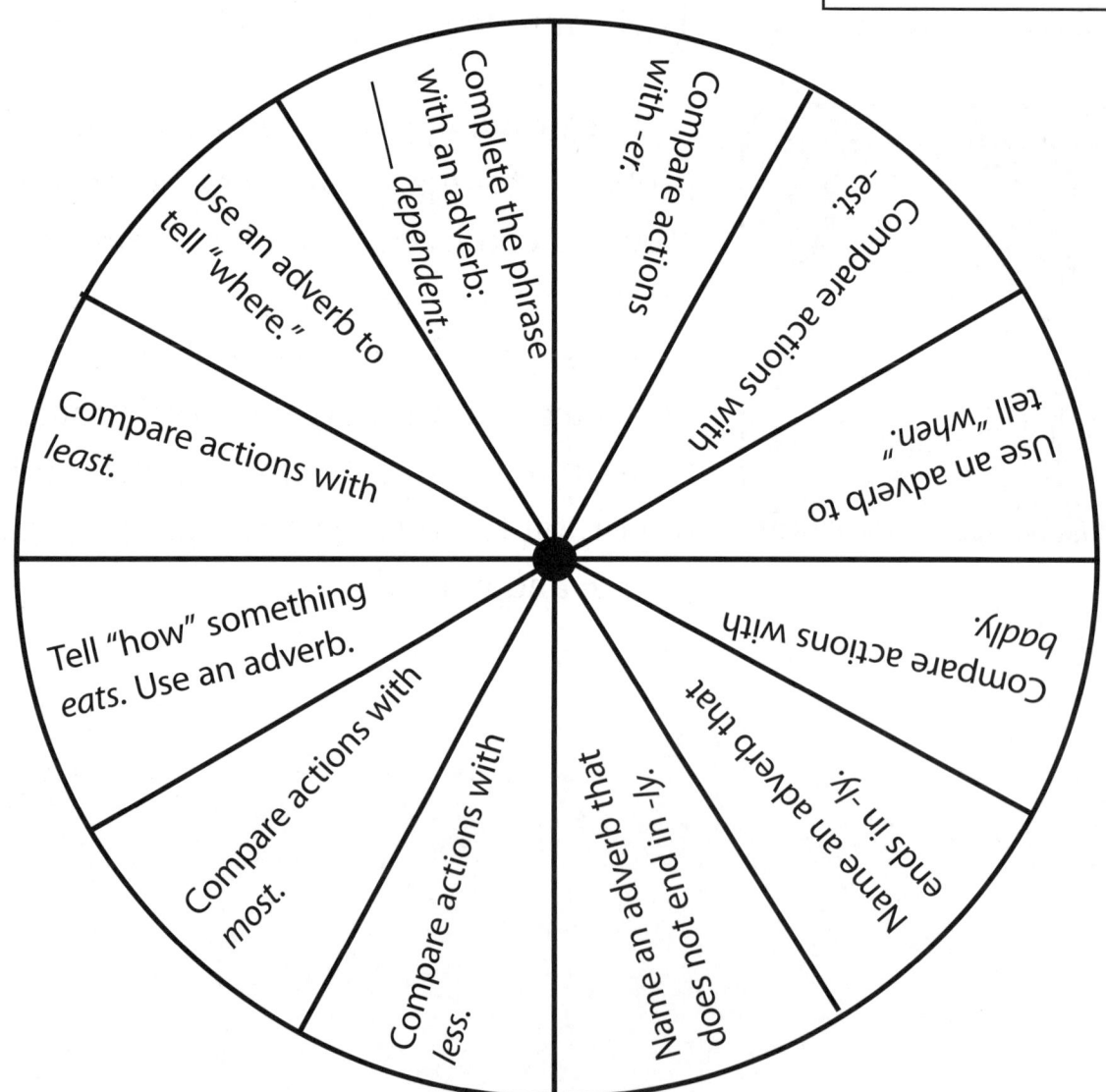

Unit 4 | Our Diverse Earth

Name _____ Date _____

Reread and Retell

"A Natural Balance"

Record text evidence and summarize the author's viewpoint in the chart.

Text evidence	Author's viewpoint
"Believe it or not, all of the things you do . . . have an impact on the world around you."	The author believes that your actions have strong, important effects on the world.

Complete the viewpoint chart. Then use the chart to summarize the main points and the author's viewpoints with a partner.

4.7

Unit 4 | Our Diverse Earth

Name _____ Date _____

Fluency

"A Natural Balance"

Use this passage to practice reading with proper phrasing.

Sometimes our actions allow a certain plant or animal population—or the	12
total number of individuals in a group—to get larger. For example, if you planted	27
tulips in your yard, the tulip population in your area would increase. Or if you	42
put seeds out for the birds in your area, the bird population might get larger.	57

Our activities also can lead to smaller plant and animal populations. 68
What would happen to the plants and animals in a neighborhood park if the 82
park were turned into an apartment building? They would either die or move 95
some place else. Then the area's plant and animal populations would shrink. 107

Overhunting, pollution, and other activities sometimes cause the 115
population of a species to become so small that it cannot survive. A species 129
that is in danger of dying out is called an endangered species. When a species 144
can no longer survive and dies out completely, it becomes extinct. A species 157
that is extinct is gone forever. 163

From "A Natural Balance," page 230

Phrasing
- [1] ☐ Rarely pauses while reading the text.
- [2] ☐ Occasionally pauses while reading the text.
- [3] ☐ Frequently pauses at appropriate points in the text.
- [4] ☐ Consistently pauses at all appropriate points in the text.

Accuracy and Rate Formula
Use the formula to measure a reader's accuracy and rate while reading aloud.

_____ − _____ = _____
words attempted   number of errors   words correct per minute
in one minute   (wcpm)

Name _____ Date _____

Reading Options

"Mireya Mayor"

Complete the chart as you read the online article.

Viewpoint	Evidence	Action needed

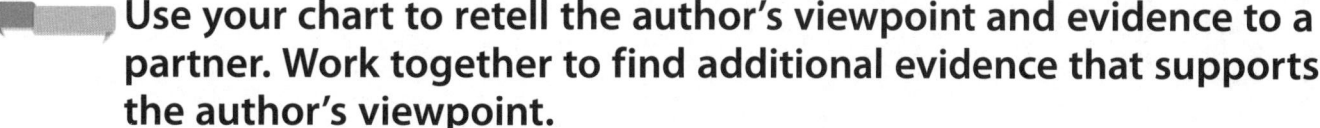 Use your chart to retell the author's viewpoint and evidence to a partner. Work together to find additional evidence that supports the author's viewpoint.

4.9

Unit 4 | Our Diverse Earth

Respond and Extend

Compare Authors' Viewpoints

Use the Venn diagram to compare authors' viewpoints.

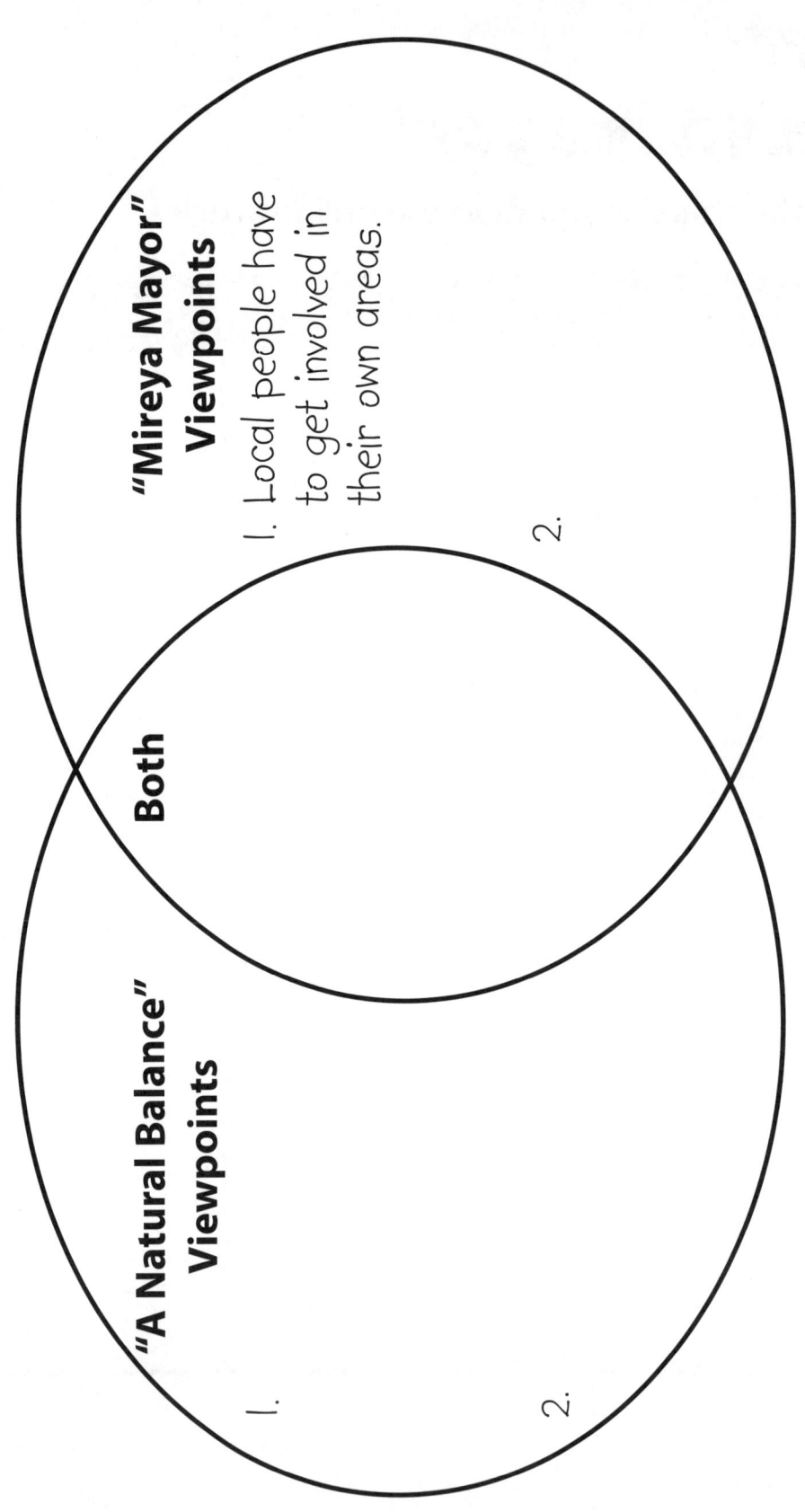

"A Natural Balance" Viewpoints
1.
2.

Both

"Mireya Mayor" Viewpoints
1. Local people have to get involved in their own areas.
2.

With a small group, discuss each text and how it expresses the author's viewpoint. What viewpoints do the two authors share? What parts of the text support these viewpoints?

Name _____ Date _____

Grammar

Mayor's Important Work

Grammar Rules: Adjectives and Adverbs

Adjectives

- Add **–er** to compare two things. Add **–est** to compare three or more things. Use **more/less** and **most/least** for adjectives with three or more syllables.
- Special forms: **good**, **better**, **best**; **bad**, **worse**, **worst**; **many**, **more**, **most**

Adverbs

- Use **more** or **less** to compare two actions with adverbs that end in **-ly**. Add **-er** to other adverbs. Use **most/least** or **–est** to compare three or more actions.
- Special forms: **well**, **better**, **best**; **badly**, **worse**, **worst**

Write the correct forms to compare. Circle the noun phrases.

1. Mouse lemurs are the _____ animals in the world.
   (small)

2. Mayor is known for researching _____ than others.
   (careful)

3. Conservation will make a _____ life for animals.
   (good)

4. Communities work _____ once Mayor educates them.
   (effective)

5. Some endangered species are _____ to save than others.
   (difficult)

Use adjectives and adverbs that compare to tell a partner about Mireya Mayor's work.

4.11 Unit 4 | Our Diverse Earth

Name _____ Date _____

Close Reading

from "Mireya Mayor," page 247

Analyze the text below with your teacher and make notes.

1   An expedition also led [Mireya] Mayor to Namibia. She went into a veterinarian's haven, or safe place, for leopards. "While caring for the leopards," Mayor explains, "the vet accidentally discovered a cure for fluid in the brain. It is a disease that also occurs in human infants. As a result of our film and the media attention it received, new studies are now taking place in children's hospitals. That is why I consider my television work just as important as my conservation field work," she notes. "The TV series sheds light on the plight of endangered species and animals around the world. Television has the power to help people know and connect with these animals and habitats that are disappearing. We may be facing the largest mass extinction of our time. Awareness is crucial. If we don't act now, it will be too late."

Name _____ Date _____

Close Reading

from "Mireya Mayor," page 248

Make notes as you read the paragraphs below. Then answer the questions on page 4.14.

1   Mayor went to Madagascar on another of her National Geographic Explorer expeditions. On that expedition, she discovered a new species of lemurs. This discovery brought everyone's attention to Mayor's work. She had to document it. Once it was documented, she could try to obtain protection for the animal's habitat. This required grueling fieldwork during the monsoon season. "There we were, tromping through remote areas of jungle, rain pouring, tents blowing. We were looking for a nocturnal animal. One that happens to be the smallest primate in the world," she says. Her careful research and documentation were important. She was able to convince Madagascar's president to declare the species' habitat a national park. Soon after that, the president also agreed to triple the number of protected areas in the nation. As Mayor reports, one tiny discovery became "a huge ambassador for all things wild in Madagascar."

Name _____ Date _____

Close Reading

from "Mireya Mayor" (continued)

Reread and annotate the passage to answer these questions.

Reread paragraph 1. Reread sentences 1–2.

1. Where did Mireya Mayor go on her expedition? Why was her lemur discovery there important? Highlight text evidence that supports your answer.

Reread sentences 3–5.

2. What did Mayor have to do to get protection for the lemur's habitat? Highlight text evidence that supports your answer.

Reread sentences 6–9.

3. Mayor claims she had to do "grueling fieldwork" on her expedition. Use text evidence to define "grueling fieldwork."

Reread sentences 10–13.

4. What happened as a result of Mayor's work with the lemurs? How did the lemurs become "huge ambassadors for all things wild in Madagascar"? Highlight text evidence that supports your answer.

Name _____ Date _____

Thinking Map

Characters' Viewpoints

Complete the character description chart.

Character	Evidence	Character's viewpoint

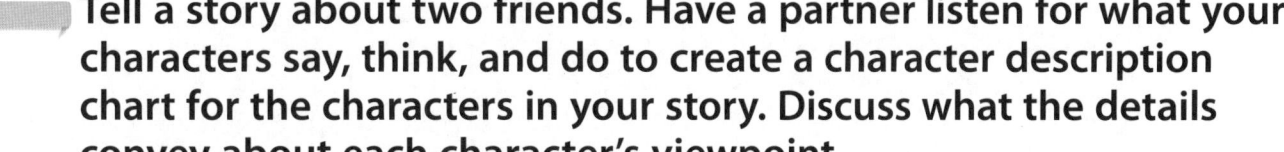 Tell a story about two friends. Have a partner listen for what your characters say, think, and do to create a character description chart for the characters in your story. Discuss what the details convey about each character's viewpoint.

Name _____   Date _____

Grammar

What Else Am I Doing?

1. With a partner, create a story about doing something good for the environment. Use **present participles**.

2. Player 1 writes a simple sentence describing what the main character is doing.

3. Player 2 spins the spinner and changes the **verb** on the spinner into a **participle**. Then Player 2 rewrites the sentence to include that participle.

4. Switch roles and repeat. Continue building on sentences to make a story.

5. Play until all of the words on the spinner have been used.

6. Share your story with the class.

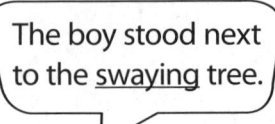
The boy stood next to the tree.

The boy stood next to the swaying tree.

Make a Spinner

1. Place one loop of a paper clip over the center of the circle.
2. Push a sharp pencil through the loop and the paper.
3. Spin the paper clip around the pencil.

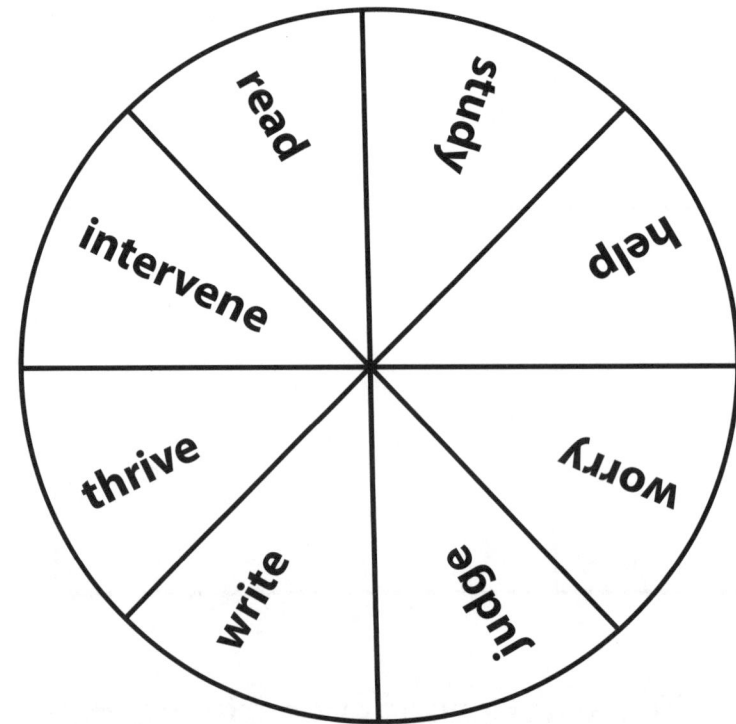

4.16   Unit 4 | Our Diverse Earth

Key Points Reading

"If Trees Could Talk"

Listen as your teacher reads. Follow with your finger.

Two Hawaiian students, Kale and Noah, get home from school one day to find a letter saying that the managers of their apartment complex are going to build a fitness center where there is now a park. They don't want to lose their park, so they decide to write a letter to tell the management company how they feel.

In their letter, Kale and Noah write about the need to protect the many species of native Hawaiian plants that live in the park. They explain that Hawaii has more than 10,000 native plant and animal species and that most of them don't live anywhere else on Earth. They present their letter to the management team.

Key Points Reading

"If Trees Could Talk" (continued)

3

Kale and Noah decide to hang a sign on a sandalwood tree in the park, explaining how important the tree is. When they come back the next day, they find that someone has added more signs. The new signs explain even more ways that the tree and the other plants around it are valuable. Kale and Noah think other residents of the apartment complex must have written the other signs.

4

Even more signs are added. After reading all the signs, the management team is convinced that the park is too valuable to build on. They decide to offer exercise classes in the park and to upgrade the existing fitness center instead of building a new one. Thanks to Kale and Noah, the park is saved.

Name _____ Date _____

Grammar

Collect the Cards

1. Play with a partner. Make sentence cards. Put the sentence cards face down in a pile.
2. Take turns. Turn over one card. Read the sentence to yourself. On a separate sheet of paper, write the sentence. Fill in the blank with the **past participle** of the verb shown in parentheses.
3. If your partner agrees that you have written the past participle correctly, keep the card. If not, put the card back at the bottom of the pile.
4. Play until all cards have been used. The player with more cards wins.

My sister will not eat _____ carrots. (cook)	Those redwoods grow in a _____ forest. (protect)
The _____ scientist appeared on T.V. (respect)	Many _____ owls live in California. (endanger)
_____, we searched the neighborhood for our dog. (worry)	We were unable to use the _____ compass. (break)
Don't touch the _____ fence. (paint)	I could not find the _____ e-mail. (delete)

4.19

Unit 4 | Our Diverse Earth

Name _____ Date _____

Reread and Explain

"If Trees Could Talk"

Complete the character description chart.

Character	Evidence	Character's viewpoint
Noah	• Noah shook his head. "That's not good news at all."	• Noah does not like the news about the park.
Kale		
Ms. Alana		

▬ Record dialogue, thoughts, and actions that support the characters' viewpoints you identify. Then explain the viewpoints to a partner.

4.20   Unit 4 | Our Diverse Earth

Fluency

"If Trees Could Talk"

Use this passage to practice reading with proper expression.

"Maybe they should hear your voices," said Kale's mom. Kale stared at the letter. "Maybe they should." — 11 / 17

Noah swallowed. "We're going to talk to the apartment managers?" "We are," said Kale. — 27 / 31

"You really think they'll listen to a couple of kids?" said Noah. — 43

"Not if we sound like clueless kids," said Kale. "They wrote a letter, so we'll write a letter back. We'll organize our thoughts on paper and then take it to the management office." — 56 / 70 / 76

Kale booted up the family computer, and he and Noah wrote their letter. They listed all the reasons the apartment complex needed the park. When they finished, Kale hit PRINT. He pulled the letter from the printer. — 88 / 100 / 113

"Ready?" said Kale. — 116

"Ready," said Noah. — 119

From "If Trees Could Talk," pages 261–262

Expression
- [1] ☐ Does not read with feeling.
- [2] ☐ Reads with some feeling, but does not match content.
- [3] ☐ Reads with appropriate feeling for most content.
- [4] ☐ Reads with appropriate feeling for all content.

Accuracy and Rate Formula
Use the formula to measure a reader's accuracy and rate while reading aloud.

_____ − _____ = _____
words attempted   number of errors   words correct per minute
in one minute   (wcpm)

Name _____ Date _____

Reading Options

"The Super Trees"

Complete the double-entry log as you read the essay.

Page	What I read	What it reminds me of

▬▬ Tell a partner which detail was most interesting and why.

Name _____ Date _____

Respond and Extend

Compare Genres

Complete the comparison chart.

	"If Trees Could Talk"	"The Super Trees"
Genre		
Main Characters or People		biologist and explorer, Mike Fay
Text Features and Forms	informal dialogue; letters and signs; illustrations	
Important Events		
Author's or Character's Viewpoint		

 With a partner, discuss each text and how each author expressed his or her viewpoint.

4.23 Unit 4 | Our Diverse Earth

Name _____ Date _____

Grammar

Mike Fay and the Redwoods

Grammar Rules: Participial Phrases

1. A **participle** or **participial phrase** acts as an adjective to describe a **noun** or **pronoun**.
2. Insert a comma (,) after a **participle** or **participial phrase** that begins a sentence.
3. Insert a comma (,) before and after a **participle** or **participial phrase** that identifies or explains the **noun** or **pronoun** that comes before it.

Read each sentence. Underline the participle or participial phrase. Some sentences may have more than one. Insert commas where they belong.

1. The sequoias standing tall and beautiful inspired Mike Fay.

2. Carrying on John Muir's work Fay fights fiercely to save the redwoods.

3. Researching intently Fay walked many miles through the protected forests of northern California.

4. Excited about his journey he talked passionately about his fascinating discoveries.

With a partner, use sentences with participles and participial phrases to tell about the ways that Mike Fay is working to save the redwood trees. Ask your partner to identify the participle or participial phrase in each sentence.

Name _____ Date _____

Close Reading

from "The Super Trees," page 280

Analyze the text below with your teacher and make notes.

1. Now, more than 100 years later, John Muir's work to save the redwoods is carried on by people like Mike Fay. It could be said that the history of modern America is carved in redwood. Mike Fay has spent three decades helping save African forests. He is a Wildlife Conservation Society biologist and National Geographic Society explorer-in-residence.

2. Mike Fay's love for the iconic American trees began a few years ago after he explored the largest intact jungle remaining in Africa. One day while driving along the northern California coast, he found himself gazing at areas of clear-cuts and spindly second-growth forests. Another time in a state park, a six-foot-tall slice of an old redwood log on display caught his attention. Near the burgundy center a label read: "1492 Columbus."

3. "The one that got me was about three inches from the edge," Fay says. "'Gold Rush, 1849.' And I realized that within the last few inches of that tree's life, we'd very nearly liquidated a 2,000-year-old forest."

4.25

Unit 4 | Our Diverse Earth

Close Reading

from "The Super Trees," page 282

Make notes as you read the paragraphs below. Then answer the questions on page 4.27.

1. Now foresters are changing to a form of single-tree selection. This is more productive in the long run than clear-cutting. Every 10 to 15 years they take about a third of the timber in a stand. They only cut down the least robust trees. This creates more open space and allows the remaining trees to get a greater share of sunlight. This also speeds their growth. Every year, the amount and quality of the standing wood increase. The process can proceed for centuries. The advantages are two-fold: short-term income and a larger payback over the long term.

2. This change isn't just about wood. Past damage to ecosystems is being repaired. Sediment is being excavated from streams to restore their flow. Trees identified as crucial for wildlife habitat are being preserved.

3. Mike Fay says, "This isn't about loving big trees. It's about the fact that I spent 333 days walking 1,800 miles through the entire range of redwoods with a notebook in my hand, documenting details about this ecosystem—and witnessing the aftermath of the cutting of at least 95 percent of the most wood-laden forest on Earth."

Name _____ Date _____

Close Reading

from "The Super Trees" (continued)

Reread and annotate the passage to answer these questions.

Reread paragraph 1.

1. What is the difference between "single-tree selection" and "clear-cutting"? Highlight text evidence that describes single-tree selection.

2. Why is single-tree selection "more productive" than clear-cutting? Highlight and use text evidence to support your answer.

3. How would there be "short-term income"? What is the "larger payback over the long term"?

Reread paragraph 2.

4. Highlight three things in this paragraph that benefit from single-tree cutting. Explain how they benefit.

Reread paragraph 3.

5. Do you think Mike Fay's work will have an impact on protecting the redwoods? Why or why not?

Name _____ Date _____

Writing Project

Organization

Writing is organized when it is easy to follow. All the ideas make sense together and flow from one idea to the next in an order that fits the writer's audience and purpose.

	Is the argument organized?	**Does the writing flow?**
4 Wow!	❑ The writing is clearly organized around a claim that is supported by reasons and evidence. ❑ The organization fits the purpose of an argument.	❑ The ideas flow smoothly and logically. ❑ The writer uses transitions to connect the claim, reasons, and evidence.
3 Ahh.	❑ The writing is mostly organized around a claim that is supported by reasons and evidence. ❑ Some evidence is vague or out of place.	❑ Most ideas flow smoothly and logically. ❑ The writer uses some transitions, but not everything is clearly connected.
2 Hmm.	❑ The writing has a claim that is supported by some reasons and evidence. ❑ A lot of the evidence is vague or out of place.	❑ The order of ideas makes some sense. ❑ The writing lacks transitions between the claim, reasons, and evidence, but I can follow what it says.
1 Huh?	❑ The writing is not organized. The writer may have forgotten to use a Claim-and-Evidence Chart.	❑ I can't tell what the writer wants to say. The writing jumps around too much.

Name _____   Date _____

Writing Project

Claim-and-Evidence Chart

Complete the chart for your argument.

Claim	Reasons and evidence	Action needed
	Reason 1: Evidence: Reason 2: Evidence:	

4.29   Unit 4 | Our Diverse Earth

Name _____   Date _____

Writing Project

Revise

Use revision marks to make changes to these paragraphs. Look for:

- reasons supported by specific, credible evidence. Do research if you need to add more.
- clear connections between claims, reasons, and evidence
- a clear statement calling for action
- formal language

Revision Marks	
∧	Add
℘	Take out
∧̓	Insert comma
/	Make lowercase

Help Local Wildlife!

Do you want to help wildlife close to home? You can support the National Wildlife Federation (NWF) in its effort to create Certified Wildlife Habitats.

The NWF needs people to create Certified Wildlife Habitats. Habitat loss is bad. A Certified Wildlife Habitat attracts animals and helps restore places for them to hang out in schoolyards like yours. Students create these habitats by providing clean water and growing plants.

You can participate in the NWF program no matter where you live. The NWF website gives you simple, step-by-step directions. Once creatures discover these wildlife-friendly places, they move right in.

Do your part. Help wildlife in your area today!

Name _____ Date _____

Writing Project

Edit and Proofread

Use revision marks to edit and proofread these paragraphs. Look for:

- correct use of adjectives and adverbs that compare
- correct use of participles and participial phrases
- places to use an appositive or a participial phrase to combine sentences
- correct use of commas, parentheses, and dashes

Revision Marks	
∧	Add
℘	Take out
∧̓	Insert comma
─∧	Insert dash
(∧	Add left parenthesis
)∧	Add right parenthesis

Partners in Conservation

Protecting American wilderness areas is not a new idea. It began with Theodore Roosevelt (President from 1901 to 1909. Roosevelt was inspired by John Muir. Muir was a dedicated naturalist.

In 1903, Roosevelt and Muir spent three nights camping in the Yosemite Valley. Using this time with the President Muir convinced Roosevelt that saving wilderness areas would be the signficantest act of his presidency. Roosevelt agreed—delighting Muir and created five new national parks. This doubled, the number of preserved national parks at the time.

The two men continued their conservation work. Muir worked even more harder than before with the Sierra Club. The Sierra Club was a group he started in 1892. However, some people believe that his partnership with Roosevelt was his goodest achievement of all.

4.31

Unit 4 | Our Diverse Earth

Photographic Credits

1.4 (t) Eye Ubiquitous/Getty Images. (b) API/Getty Images. 1.5 (t) Keystone-France/Getty Images. (b) Bettmann/Getty Images. 2.4 (t, c) ROBERT SISSON/National Geographic Image Collection. (b) ROBERT E. HYNES/National Geographic Image Collection. 3.4 (t) Danita Delimont/Alamy Stock Photo. (c) Barry Iverson/The LIFE Images Collection/Getty Images. (b) Kenneth Garrett/National Geographic Image Collection. 4.4 SKIP BROWN/National Geographic Image Collection. 4.5 (t) Joseph Van Os/The Image Bank/Getty Images. (b) Joel Sartore/National Geographic Image Collection.